Soliloquy Prayer

Soliloquy *Prayer*

Unfolding Our Hearts to God

DENNIS BILLY, C.Ss.R.

Liguori

LIGUORI, MISSOURI

Published by Liguori Publications
Liguori, Missouri

Library of Congress Cataloging-in-Publication Data

Billy, Dennis, J., C.Ss.R.
    Soliloquy prayer : unfolding our hearts to God / Dennis J. Billy. — 1st ed.
       p. cm.
    ISBN 0-7648-0222-4
    1. Prayer—Catholic Church. 2. Bible. O.T. Psalms—Devotional use. 3. Catholic Church—Prayer-books and devotions—English. I. Title.
BV215.B55 1998
248.3—dc21   98–20160

Printed in the United States of America
02 01 00 99 98 5 4 3 2 1
First Edition

In loving Memory of Madeleine Rignault

(1912–1991)

———————

So I always desire to say in this life so I wish to die,
breathing forth my last sigh with this dear word on my lips,
"My God, I love you!"

Alphonsus de Liguori,
The Practice of the Love of Jesus Christ

Acknowledgments

ALL SCRIPTURAL CITATIONS in the body of the text come from *The New American Bible* (New York: Catholic Book Publishing, Co., 1991). Scriptural citations in the appendices are from the *New Revised Standard Version of the Bible*, copyright 1989 by the Division of Christian Education of the National Council of Churches of the USA; used with permission.

Other citations come from: Aelred of Rievaulx, *Spiritual Friendship*, trans. Mary Eugenia Laker, Cistercian Fathers Series 5 (Kalamazoo, MI: Cistercian Publications, 1977), 131; Albert and Thomas, *Selected Writings*, ed. and trans. Simon Tugwell, The Classics of Western Spirituality (New York/Mahwah: Paulist Press, 1988), 481; Alan of Lille, *The Art of Preaching*, trans. Gillian R. Evans, Cistercian Studies Series 23 (Kalamazoo, MI: Cistercian Publications, 1981), 108; Bonaventure, *The Soul's Journey into God, The Tree of Life, The Life of St. Francis*, trans. Ewert Cousins, The Classics of Western Spirituality (New York/Ramsey/Toronto: Paulist Press, 1978), 67-68; Catherine of Genoa, *Purgation and Purgatory, The Spiritual Dialogue*, trans. Serge Hughes, The Classics of Western Spirituality (New York/Ramsey/Toronto: Paulist Press, 1979), 119; Catherine of Siena, *The Dialogue*, trans. Suzanne Noffke, The Classics of Western Spirituality (New York/Ramsey/Toronto: Paulist Press, 1980), 141–42; Hadewijch, *The Complete Works*, trans. Mother Columba Hart, The Classics of Western Spirituality (New York/Ramsey/Toronto: Paulist Press, 1980), 113; Hildegard of Bingen, *Scivias*, trans. Columba Hart and Jane Bishop, The Classics of Western Spirituality (New York/Mahwah: Paulist

Press, 1990), 87; John Ruusbroec, *The Spiritual Esposals and Other Works*, trans. James A. Wiseman, The Classics of Western Spirituality (New York/Ramsey/Toronto: Paulist Press, 1985), 68; Julian of Norwich, *Showings*, trans. Edmund Colledge and James Walsh, The Classics of Western Spirituality (New York/Ramsey/Toronto: Paulist Press, 1978), 142–43; Teresa of Ávila, *The Interior Castle*, trans. Kieran Kavanaugh and Otilio Rodriguez, The Classics of Western Spirituality (New York/Ramsey/Toronto: Paulist Press, 1979), 40; Thomas Spidlik, *Drinking from the Hidden Fountain: A Patristic Breviary, Ancient Wisdom for Today's World*, trans. Paul Drake, Cistercian Studies Series 148 (Kalamazoo, MI/Spencer, MA: Cistercian Publications, 1994), 37–38, 289; Walter Hilton, *The Scale of Perfection*, trans. John P. H. Clark and Rosemary Dorward, The Classics of Western Spirituality (Mahwah: Paulist Press, 1991), 232; William of St. Thierry, *The Golden Epistle*, trans. Theodore Berkeley, Cistercian Fathers Series 12 (Spencer MA: Cistercian Publications, 1971), 18.

Contents

Prayer to Jesus

Guide my hand, Lord,
As I open my heart
And try to convey
In words
What my experience
Of you
Has been like.
Help me to listen
To the movement
Of your Spirit
In my heart,
And to express
What I find there
Openly and honestly—
Without holding anything back.
Help me,
Most of all,
To praise you,
To thank you,
And to turn to you
With all my
Heart, mind, soul, and strength!
To you be given
All glory, praise, and honor
Both on earth
And in the heavens
Forever and ever!
Amen.

*I*ntroduction

THINK BACK TO another time in your life.

- When did you first learn how to pray?
- What is your earliest recollection of praying?
- How old were you? Who were you with?
- What did you say? How did you say it?

It is difficult going back through our memories in order to pinpoint an exact time or place for the beginning of what is arguably the most important activity any of us will ever do in life. It is not unlike trying to remember when we learned how to talk. Unless we were told about it at a later date, few of us have any recollection of the circumstances surrounding our first spoken words. We simply listened, watched, learned— and made plenty of mistakes! Eventually, we got the hang of making sounds into spoken words.

Learning to Pray

Just as we learned to talk by mimicking others, most of us also learned how to pray by imitating those around us. This imitation came about in any number of ways—when our father bobbed us on his knee and playfully led us through the sign of the cross; when our mother reverently bowed her head and talked to God with us before she tucked us in for the night; when we went to church on Sunday and followed the lead of the people around us, doing what they did, when they did it, and exactly how they did it. We learned how to pray by following the example of others. We imitated them and followed their every move. Through constant repetition, the words and the motions gradually became our own. This process continued even as our speech patterns became more sophisticated and as we learned how to express ourselves with more nuance and greater proficiency.

"Lord, teach us how to pray" (Lk 11:1). Even Jesus' closest disciples felt the need to imitate him, to learn from him an approach to prayer that would deepen the way they conversed with God. How much more should we follow in their footsteps! We need to pose this humble request for guidance in prayer not once, but every day of our lives—and many times each day! This request is the simplest and purest of prayers—so easy to say and, yet, so easy to forget. Without it, the disciples never would have received from Jesus his most precious and cherished gift, the freedom to call God "Father." Without it, we never would have been able to address God on such intimate terms and express our needs in ways undreamed of by our human minds.

Rediscovering the Soliloquy

What you have before you is a book of prayers known as "soliloquies." Soliloquies are a once popular but now very much neglected form of prayer, whose main purpose is to help us to improve the texture and quality of our ongoing conversation with God. Why this neglect? Many of us have simply forgotten how to communicate to God in the deeply affectionate and intimate terms used in these prayers, quite possibly because, for a variety of personal and cultural factors, we no longer experience God as a vital, personal presence in our lives. A return to the soliloquy may help to awaken this sense of deep, heartfelt intimacy with a personal God. The soliloquy filled this role of creating spiritual intimacy for many of our religious forebears; it might very well do the same for us. The following points of inquiry should help us to understand why.

What Is A Soliloquy Prayer?

Soliloquies are first-person narrative prayers of various lengths whose purpose is to draw the pray-er into an intimate personal union with God. Autobiographical in nature, but imbued with a strong universal appeal, soliloquies are a confirmation of the traditional spiritual insight that the most private of matters are often concerns that are often shared by all humans. As a prayer form, soliloquies combine strong rhetorical flair with deep childlike trust to penetrate the mystery of the framer's relationship with God.

This conversational understanding of prayer (that is, plain, heartfelt talking to God) bridges the ever-widening gap in today's religious arena between traditional forms of devotional prayer (for example, the rosary, novenas, the Stations of the Cross, and so on) and contemplation (for example, centering prayer, the prayer of quiet, Zen meditation). Although, strictly speaking, soliloquies fall into the category of meditations (that is, reflections of the mind oriented toward God), they can also be prayed aloud and even with one's spirit in an entirely interior way (1 Th 5:23). In this respect, they can help us to integrate *oratio* (vocal prayer), *meditatio* (mental prayer), and *contemplatio* (contemplation) in a single experience of heartfelt prayer (See the *Catechism of the Catholic Church*, 1994, paragraphs 2700-2724).

At their best, soliloquies engage the *whole* person in prayer and invite him or her to do the same in his or her relationship with others. The delicate balance soliloquies maintain between piercing intellectual prowess and powerful affective imagery presumes no false division between head and heart, but invites the persons praying of the prayer to enter into the words completely and to take seriously the Gospel injunction to love God with all one's heart, soul, mind, and strength (Mk 12:30).

Development of Soliloquy Prayer

Soliloquies have deep roots in the Christian spiritual tradition and have undergone a great deal of internal development. In the beginning, they were very loosely structured, spontaneous heartfelt outpourings, which the originators sometimes committed to writing to benefit themselves and perhaps a small group of intimate friends. As these written-down versions of soliloquies were disseminated and grew in popularity, they gradually became longer and began to take on a recognizable structure that incorporated a threefold movement within this prayer format of thanksgiving, praise, and petition. Because they were often read aloud for the benefit of those who could not read, soliloquies used simple language, a repetitious style, and short ejaculatory prayers as a means of helping the memory. "Thank you, Lord," "Praise you, Lord," and "Help me, Lord," were common refrains that could be found in each soliloquy and could be carried beyond it, outside the allotted time set aside for formal prayer.

The original simple style of soliloquies lent itself to a deep emotional expression which remained an integral part of this prayer form even as the audience for these types of prayers became more and more literate and the structure of the soliloquy became more highly refined. This process of development reached its climax in the rigorous concern for method that marked many of the post-Tridentine approaches to mental prayer. What many of these highly developed systems of prayer gained, however, by way of careful step-by-step instructions in the spiritual life, was often lost on account of the very tight reins they kept on the feelings. Their programmed mistrust of and, at times, outright neglect of the emotions fostered a fragmented (one might go so far as to say "dichotomized") understanding of the human person that would haunt popular Catholic spirituality for generations to come.

One noticeable exception to this neglect of the emotions in spiritual life was the approach to mental prayer presented in the ascetical works of Saint Alphonsus de Liguori (1696–1787). This great doctor of prayer taught that everyone receives enough grace to pray and that prayer was the ordinary means given to us by God for our salvation. "If you pray, you will certainly be saved," he liked to say. Deeply aware of the psychology of the person at prayer, Alphonsus made sure to give the emotions a prominent place in his presentation of mental prayer. His steps included:

(1) the preparation, where one disposes both mind and body to enter into a state of recollection;

(2) the meditation, where one reflects in silence upon a passage from Scripture or a book of spiritual readings;

(3) the affections, where one raises the heart to God with acts of humility, thanksgiving, contrition, and love;

(4) the petitions, where one asks God for grace to lead a devout and holy life;

(5) the resolution, where one decides on a concrete and practical course of action for the day; and

(6) a conclusion, where one gives thanks to God, asks for the grace to fulfill the resolution that was made, and to remain faithful to Jesus and Mary.

Alphonsus' genius in this presentation of mental prayer lies in the way he combines the spontaneity of the original soliloquy form with the pointed concerns of his day for structure and method. A reading of any one of the hundreds upon hundreds of affections and acts of love that fill his ascetical works shows that, with Alphonsus, the soliloquy prayer has reached an important hallmark in its development. The precipitous decline of the soliloquy in later years stemmed, at least in part, from the breakup of the very delicate balance that Alphonsus had achieved.

Soliloquy Prayer and the Psalms

This book is an attempt to recover the soliloquy for an age that has long since forgotten this prayer form. To do so, we must go back to an earlier stage in its development as a type of prayer, when the spontaneous outpouring of the heart counted for much more than the loosely organized structure of thanksgiving, praise, and petition in which it was embedded. This examination of the soliloquy's origin means that we must go back long before the time of the delicate balance achieved by Alphonsus to the time when the soliloquy was little more than the spontaneous revelation of a person's most intimate thoughts and feelings to God. This look at the origins of the soliloquy should be a welcome relief to those who have become "put off" by Western culture's compulsive attachment to method. It also should encourage persons taking up this prayer format to look at the ways they currently relate to God to see if they are trying to hide something or to hold something back from the source of all and the ground of all being.

The fifteen soliloquies in this volume get their inspiration from the Book of Psalms. That is not to say that they are commentaries on the psalms or that they offer original insights into their makeup and meaning. It means only that the opening psalm at each of the book's fifteen chapters serves as the official point of departure for the intense, personal prayer that follows. The connection between the psalm and the soliloquy is sometimes obvious and sometimes not. To highlight this connection, a brief meditation from a well-known

Catholic saint or mystic has been placed between them to serve as a theological and spiritual bridge.

The use of the psalms in this manner is appropriate, not only because they themselves closely resemble the literary style of the soliloquy (and may, in fact, have inspired it), but also because they lend themselves to a variety of interpretations (for example, private or communal, or interpretations using Christ, the human soul, the Church, or the last things as reference points). When taken together, the fifteen psalms that have been selected offer a wide range of deeply religious sentiments: suffering, awe, thanksgiving, uncertainty, faith, hope—to name just a few. Like the Psalter from which they were taken, they do not follow a predetermined pattern of progression but represent a loosely connected ensemble of hymns and canticles that touch on some of the most heartfelt of all religious convictions.

Inspired by these psalms, the soliloquies themselves provide a detailed collage of the believer at prayer. They, too, are self-contained units and can be read in whatever order one desires. When taken together, they provide a choice library of intimate conversations with God which, though similar in form, unveil different, even conflicting, thoughts, attitudes, and emotions of great religious import. The purpose of this self-disclosure is not to inform God of something yet unknown, but to enable the person at prayer to get in touch with and comprehend where he or she stands in relationship to God. These soliloquies also serve as a model for those who wish to attempt this prayer format on their own, or who wish to take off on their own after a few promptings from the written soliloquy. In this way, the soliloquies invite you to devise your own prayers couched in this form and to deepen your own self-understanding, a necessary requisite for anyone who wishes to draw closer to God.

The Soliloquy As an Aid to Prayer

As with most prayers, we learn how to pray soliloquies by following the lead of others, in this case, people who are especially gifted with the ability to put down in writing the innermost thoughts they express to God. Like any other prayers, these written soliloquies are texts to be used for imitation, not as subjects for analysis or intense critical scrutiny. In this case, simply read them in a quiet, prayerful manner and let the Spirit of God do its work. Soliloquies reveal a person's heartfelt conversation with God. By writing the words down on paper, some people are able to enter more deeply into that conversation and thus come to a fuller understanding of his or her relationship with God. When going through the soliloquies in this book or others that have been recorded in print, the reader receives the opportunity to address God in a similar way, either by adapting the words of the soliloquy itself or by using words of his or her own making. In either case, the soliloquy helps people to conceive of their relationship with God in the deepest, most affectionate, and most intimate terms possible. Since many people have a difficult time doing this on their own, the prepared text can help them to imagine the kind of intimacy they are called to enjoy with God.

The soliloquy is an instrument for fostering deeper intimacy with God: nothing more; nothing less. Its words should not be adhered to slavishly or interfere with other, perhaps equally effective forms of prayer. It seeks not to replicate the writer's relationship with God in the reader, or to canonize it, but to give the reader the opportunity to gaze upon one person's intimate conversation with God and to experience appropriate language for effecting something similar in his or her own life.

Readers of soliloquies that have been put into writing can use these models in a variety of ways:

(1) They can undertake an extended act of the imagination that adopts the mind-set or "persona" of the author as the words are prayed;

(2) They can follow the words of the soliloquy through, either quietly or aloud, and stop at those places in the text where the words touch their own inner experience; or

(3) They can use the soliloquy as a way of settling down and entering into the proper frame of mind so that they can write down or simply converse with God in their own intimate terms.

However one decides to use the model soliloquies, the reader must remember to bring his or her whole person to the activity of prayer. A mere recitation of the words is not enough. Something more is required.

Prayer is not so much an activity we do, but something God does in us. We do not *construct* our relationship with God—be it through words, ideas, or expressions—but we are invited to participate in it. The words we pray, our own or those of others, are only external expressions of what God does within us. Everything else is purely secondary.

How to Pray the Soliloquy Prayers

To enable you to enter more deeply into the spirit of these prayers, each of the fifteen soliloquies in this book has been couched in a six-part structure that includes:

(1) an introduction to the topic under consideration;

(2) a few short verses from the psalm that inspired it;

(3) a brief meditation from a well-known saint or mystic of the Catholic tradition that offers some insight into the theological presuppositions that guide what is to follow;

(4) the soliloquy itself;

(5) a series of reflection questions aimed to help you unravel the meaning of the soliloquy and to formulate your own questions to put to God; and

(6) a brief exercise to help you to digest those questions and enter into your own intimate conversation with God.

Although this structure is carefully thought-out to maximize your appreciation of each soliloquy, please feel free to utilize it as you see fit. This structure is meant only as an aid to prayer. If you find that it is not useful and, in some cases, even distracting, please feel free to rearrange or even ignore it. Taken alone, the soliloquies themselves should offer you more than enough for your own fruitful reflection.

For those wishing to follow the structure provided, however, a number of observations are in order. In the first place, the verses of the psalm normally represent only a part of the entire hymn. If time and inclination permit, it is suggested that you keep a Bible by your side so that at appropriate moments in your reading and reflection, you may refer to the psalm in its entirety. This further reading of the psalm will enable you to enter more deeply into the meaning of the psalm itself and to draw further connections with what is to follow. This extended reading could also be done for the brief passage that follows each psalm, although these are usually self-contained quotations that are more readily understood in their own right.

As far as the soliloquy itself is concerned, try to go through the text once all the way to get a sense of its movement, length, and pace. Then go over it a second time, stopping at those places that are particularly meaningful to you and where you need to stop and reflect. Put the book down, if necessary, and let your heart and mind follow the inspiration of the moment. There is no need to return to the text; it will be there when you return. Remember, the book is meant to be a help to you in prayer. It is not a book to be read from cover to cover in a single sitting, but a series of meditations and exercises that a person takes up and returns to again and again at various moments in his or her life.

As far as the reflection questions are concerned, read them once through carefully, but do not try to answer all of them all at once. One or two will do for the present moment; the others will give you something to reflect on when you return to the book at a later date. The exercise at the end of each chapter, moreover, is also only a suggestion. It may or may not be appropriate for you when you come to it. If you find it is not, try to think up your own exercise, one that will help you talk to God from the heart about things that truly matter to you.

Finally, try to get the most out of one soliloquy before you move on to the next. Follow them in whatever order you choose. What does not suit you today may very well do so tomorrow. You may even want to read them out loud or try writing some of your own before you decide to move on. Then you would truly be praying by way of imitation. Go ahead. Try it. What's there to be afraid of? You have nothing to lose and everything to gain!

Conclusion

It would be foolish to suggest that everyone will find themselves attracted to the soliloquy as a way of conversing with God. Some will benefit greatly from it; others, much less; still others, hardly at all. Such a judgment points not to its inadequacies as a form of prayer, but only to the fact that differing personalities and psychological needs lead people to favor certain forms of prayer over others.

This assertion, however, should not prevent the bold and adventuresome from responding to the noble challenge that this book presents to their powers of imagination. The retrieval of the soliloquy as a form of prayer may well serve as a beacon in a dark age of uncertainty for all those in search of a deep, personal relationship with God. Why? Because it reminds those who have somehow forgotten how close, intimate friends actually converse with one another. Such is the relationship with God offered by the Christian faith: "I no longer call you slaves.... I have called you friends" (Jn 15:15).

Close friends dwell in each other's hearts. The soliloquies in this book reveal something of the deep, intimate relationship with God that each of us is called to share. Despite their shortcomings (and there are many), they hold nothing back from God and fully expect God to do the same. Jesus himself showed us this when he taught us to call God "Abba," "Father," and to bring to him our every need. What more can be said? Everything he thought, said, and did flowed from this one basic relationship. What he stood for and how he died can hardly be understood otherwise.

Soliloquy Prayer

Contrary Voices

Introduction

What is it like to believe in the midst of uncertainty? How can we deal with the faint whisperings of doubt that speak to us even during our deepest and most solemn acts of worship? How can we be men and women of faith when nearly everything around us speaks to us otherwise?

The first soliloquy takes a hard look at the inner dialogue between faith and doubt that goes on in the mind of nearly every believer, most especially at the end of an old, and the dawn of a new, millennium. This soliloquy does so not resort to pat answers or attempt to resolve this dilemma by pretending that a tension does not exist, but it simply acknowledges to ourselves—and to God—that both the voice of faith and the voice of doubt lay claim to our lives and are constantly vying for our attention. All we, as believers, can do is to be honest with God and take the risk of sharing both sides of our experience with him. He who formed our innermost being understands the complexity of our hearts.

Psalm

You formed my inmost being;
*   you knit me in my mother's womb.*
I praise you, so wonderfully you made me;
*   wonderful are your works!*
My very self you knew;
*   my bones were not hidden from you,*

When I was being made in secret,
*   fashioned as in the depths of the earth.*
Your eyes foresaw my actions;
*   in your book all are written down;*
*   my days were shaped, before one came to be.*
                                        Psalm 139:13–16

Meditation

It should be kept in mind here that the fount, the shin-
ing sun that is in the center of the soul, does not lose its
beauty and splendor; it is always present in the soul,
and nothing can take away its loveliness. But if a black
cloth is placed over a crystal that is the sun, obviously
the sun's brilliance will have no effect on the crystal even
though the sun is shining on it.
            Teresa of Ávila, *The Interior Castle*, 1.2.3

Soliloquy Prayer

I am impelled to write of you, my Lord, and to tell others of
your greatness. But words are so inadequate, and I do not
know where to begin. You are present in all things, in all
circumstances, in all events. Even time and space respond to
the movement of your gentle, guiding hands. You are here,
everywhere: above me, below me, before me, behind me,
within me. The same is also true for every person I will ever
meet and not meet, for all those born ages before me, and
long after me. Everyone upon whom your sun rises and sets
bears the mark of your inestimable glory. You have brought
all of us into existence and will one day call each of us home.

All the world proclaims your greatness: every animal
and plant, every rock and tree, every brook and stream, every mountain and valley, every ocean and sea, the entire sky

above and all the earth below. Men, women, and children of every religion, of every race, of every nation, long for the day when they will see you face to face. But what will they see on such a day? Will their days of longing finally be at an end? Or will they continue to search for the fulfillment of their deepest hopes.

Lord, I want to believe; I yearn to believe; I cry to believe. But strange, contrary voices assail me from all sides and give me little time for rest. They are voices of which my elders were only faintly aware. "Who do you think you are? Upon what pretense do you dare speak on such intimate terms with God? Do you presume to know what you do not know, to move that which cannot be moved, to set ablaze that which burns only from within?"

Even as I write them, my words crumble against a towering wall of uncertainty. Sentence by sentence, word by word, sound by sound, my deeply rooted insecurities pick the flesh off the decaying carcass of my once strongly held beliefs. I believe yet believe not; know yet know not; yearn yet yearn not. Boredom fills the greatest part of my waking hours; incessant doubts and questionings follow close behind.

I find myself out of touch with all I once held so dear. Family, friends, relatives. I know them, but know them not. I know myself, yet am even more a stranger to myself. My relationships are constantly shifting. Nothing is constant, nothing remains the same—not even my faith. Words come slowly or not at all. I look to the sky, take a breath, and ponder the mystery of a world teeming with life.

Lord, the world I live in teaches me to believe in you and not to believe in you. I believe with my mind and part of my heart; at other times, with my heart and part of my mind; at still other times, with no heart and with no mind. But this belief and disbelief is all a contradiction in terms. How can I believe in you and not believe in you? How can I cut my mind off from the intuitions of my heart or cut my heart off from the insights of my mind? How can I be mindless or heartless and still call myself a believer?

You, O Lord, know me through and through. You know my weaknesses and my strengths, my tendency toward good and my propensities toward evil. You knew me before my parents knew me, before my closest friends and companions knew me, before I even knew myself and was even aware that I had a self. What is more, you knew from all eternity all that I would ever do or aspire to be: my every thought, my every action; my every success, my every failure. You knew what I would think of you, when I would rebel from you, when I would return to you and speak to you.

You know everything about me, Lord, and I know so very, very little of you. Why do you hide from me? Why do you refuse to speak to me? I cry to you at all times and yet hear no answer. What have I done to deserve your silent rebuffs? Am I deaf to your ways? Are your words too eloquent for my simple ears? Have I become too complacent with myself to listen intently for your challenging words?

I speak to you, Lord, and soon find myself having nothing more to say. Only then, when all my words are spent can I linger in the surrounding silence and sense your presence in the quiet of my heart. You speak to me, Lord. But your words are strange and they require time to listen and learn their meaning. They require patience to rest in the present moment, and time to believe in the coming of one who always comes to us—where we are, as we are, when we are.

I cannot rush your coming. Lord, I cannot dictate the movement of your hand in the lives of your people. I am beginning to see that to hear you, to discern your presence in my midst, to be with you at all times and to be held by your warm embrace, I need to let go of my expectations of who you are, of how you come, and how you speak to the human heart.

I need to release you from my image of you, and allow you to come in your own time, and in your own choosing. Only then will I be free to recognize you in the unexpected as well as in the ordinary. Only then will I be open enough to allow you to lead me as you see fit. I begin to see what must be done, Lord, and yet am saddened by my incapacity to change. You already know this, Lord, but it does me good to admit this and to do so often. Otherwise I will end up deceiving myself—and others in the process.

I am humbled by your care and concern for us, Lord. But just what is it that you expect from us? How can we, who have received everything from you give you anything back in return? There is nothing we possess that does not come from your own hands—nothing but our innermost desires and the deepest affections of our hearts. Is that all you wish, O Lord? Is that why you have created the universe and everything in it? Is that why you created us and have given so very, very much to us?

The ramblings of my heart have taught me to look for you, Lord, not so much in my goals and destinations, but in the in-between times and places that take me to them. There you are, as you always have been, a quiet traveling companion who accompanies us on our journey through life. There you are, Lord, in those pregnant moments of waiting that fill so much of our lives with quiet expectation. You, who taught us the meaning of passion, are with us as we face our own day-to-day trials. You it is who taught us how to wait. You it is who showed us the meaning of quiet anticipation and who promises to show us the deeper and fuller meaning of time.

Lord, my walk with you is a walk in the darkness: I do not know for sure where I am going; at times I seriously doubt if it is even you who are leading me. To walk in hope through the darkness of life is to experience the profound depths of one's own being. May this knowledge of self, O Lord, lead me to a deeper and more intimate knowledge of you. May it help me to plumb the depths of that mystery, your mystery, in whose image I have been and am still being made. So may it be and one day come to pass.

Reflection Questions

1. How would you describe your relationship with God? Do you talk to God regularly?
2. Do you have an intimate relationship with God? Do you believe that God has a plan for your life?
3. Can you share anything you want with God, your struggles as well as your joys and hopes?
4. Do you believe that you have been put on this earth for a purpose? Do you know what it is? If so, have you been able to fulfill it? If not, how can you go about discerning it?
5. Do you have any doubts about your faith? How do you deal with them? Ignore them? Repress them? Pretend they do not exist? Do you admit them? Do you stare them in the eye? Do you bring them to God?
6. Do you ask God for help? What kind of help do you ask for?

Exercise

Make a list of all of your doubts about your faith. Make another list of all of your secrets, the things that you keep from others, that you are ashamed of, that no one else knows about. Think hard. Take your time. Make the list as long as necessary. When you have finished, take the list with you to a quiet place. Light a candle and raise your heart and your mind to God. Read the list out, slowly, one item at a time. After each entry say, "Help me, Lord, help me." When you have finished reading out the list, spend a few more moments in silence. Then take the list and burn it in the flame of the candle.

Soliloquy Prayer 2

The World Around Me

Introduction

One of the few certain things in life is the world we live in. Each of us has been born into it and will one day leave it. We wake up to it each and every day and live out our lives against the backdrop of its constant, ongoing presence. Without the world to sustain us and nurture us none of us would be here. For this reason alone, our ties with the natural world must be numbered among our most fundamental relationships.

The next soliloquy looks at our attitudes toward the world which may have led us to take it for granted and, at times, even to abuse it. It acknowledges our failings before God and humbly asks his help in changing those destructive tendencies to which we have succumbed. It also asks for guidance in discerning what we can do to right the wrongs we have committed and to make our world a better place. The world we live in is the only one we have. If we do not care for it, it will no longer be able to provide for us. We, as a result, will be hurting ourselves and many other creatures in the process if we ignore this responsibility.

Psalm

You made springs flow into channels
that wind among the mountains.
They give drink to every beast of the field;
here wild asses quench their thirst.

Beside them the birds of heaven nest;
   from among the branches they sing.
You water the mountains from your palace;
   by your labor the earth abounds.
You raise grass for the cattle
   and plants for our beasts of burden.
You bring bread from the earth,
   and wine to gladden our hearts.

Psalm 104:10–15

Meditation

Whoever, therefore, is not enlightened by such splendor of created things is blind; whoever is not awakened by such outcries is deaf; whoever does not praise God because of all of these effects is dumb; whoever does not discover the First Principle from such clear signs is a fool. Therefore, open your eyes, alert the ears of your spirit, open your lips and apply your heart so that in all creatures you may see, hear, praise, love and worship, glorify and honor your God lest the whole world rise against you.

Bonaventure, The Soul's Journey into God, 1.15

Soliloquy Prayer

How can I say I love you, Lord, when I treat your creation so carelessly and with so little respect? How can I turn to you in prayer when I turn away from the abuse my own indifference has brought to your land? How can I walk this earth, eat, drink, and clothe myself from its produce without averting to the terrible treatment this earth has received at the hands of your people?

Down through the years, my awareness of my relationship to the world and its environment has been very slight, almost negligible. For some reason, it never figured much in my religious consciousness. I considered the resources of the world something I could use at will, as beneficial rights or privileges given to me and to the rest of humanity to do with as we pleased. I used the environment for my own advantage. I was taught to do this, almost from the cradle, not consciously so, but as an unspoken assumption about the way things were.

We assumed that the world was put here for our benefit. We were called to subdue it and to have dominion over it. We were taught to take from the world and give back nothing in return. The world was ours to do with as we saw fit. Sadly, we are now paying the terrible price for our gross negligence and lack of foresight. The world is slowly running out of resources to support the human population. The survival of the planet is now at risk, and there seems very little time for decisive action.

But how can I change attitudes and modes of behavior that have been embedded in me for my entire life? How can I root out the tendencies that damage rather than build up the world in which I live? How can I right the wrongs I have participated in and which now overwhelm me and seem so far beyond my control? I ask for your help, Lord. I have often asked for it in the past and will doubtless do so many times in the future. I need you beside me as I face the tough choices ahead about the way I have compromised my relationship to the environment.

Help me, Lord, to remain true to your teaching. Help me to find vestiges of your presence in the world around me. Help me to protect what I find and not allow it to be marred by the scars of human and industrial waste. Be with me as I attempt to make small changes in my relationship to your creation. Show me the best and most appropriate steps to be taken. Help me to be patient with those steps and to be consistent when applying them to concrete situations. Help me also to be persistent in my efforts and to persevere until the end.

I see the difficulty in what I ask of you, Lord. My attitudes and behavior are intricately tied up with structures and ideologies over which I have very little control. I am a victim of my social environment as much as I am an agent in it. Even when I act alone, my actions are shaped by the thought patterns and concerns of the culture in which I live. While I do not discount my ability to interact with the world around me and to make a difference in it, I am keenly aware of the reciprocal effect that society has on me and the great extent to which I am shaped by the questions posed to me.

Still, I recognize that whatever impact I make will be insignificant if it is not done in concert with your providential will. Without your help, Lord, I will not be able to rise to the occasion and see what needs to be done to free the world from human oppression. Without your help, Lord, I will not be able to do what needs to be done once I see it. You are my help in times of need. You are humanity's help in times of need. You are all the world's help in times of need. Come to us. Help us. Show us the way and teach us how to walk it.

It is a much bigger question, Lord, than simply what I can personally accomplish to better the world I live in. I also must take into account my understanding of you and your relationship with the world, as well as my understanding of the world and its relationship with me and the rest of the human family. To recognize what must be done, I need to take a good, hard look at the relationships existing between nature, you, and humanity. In examining these ties, I need to be guided by the quiet movement of your Spirit in my heart. Only through prayerful discernment will I come to an adequate understanding of what I need to do.

Help me, Lord, to bring these concerns to you in prayer. Help me to probe the depths of the relationships among all your creatures. Help me to understand more deeply their relationship to you. You are Lord of all that exists! The heavens, the seas, the earth, the skies, the mountains and hills, the rivers and streams, the deserts and plains, the forests and fields all give you glory and proclaim your greatness. Do not let me get in the way of this great hymn of praise. Do not let me tarnish the voices of your creatures as they praise you.

I love you, Lord, and because of that love I love all the creatures who fill this world. Help me to understand my role in this great universe of yours. Help me to understand and to carry out my responsibilities in a way that conforms to the dignity you have bestowed on me. Help me to turn to you in times of trouble, and help me always to place your will for me and for the world before my own personal agenda or private self-interests.

I turn to you, Lord, and ask you to help me to care for the world. Teach me to be conscious of the vast interrelated nature of the world and everything in it. Help me to live my life in harmony with my social and environmental surroundings. Do not let me be overwhelmed by the immensity of the problems before me. Do not let me get discouraged or exceedingly anxious about the future.

Help me to work hard to resolve the tense situations I find myself in and to trust that you, who promised never to abandon me, will be there for me in my time of need. Help me, Lord, help me. The problems are great, but my hope in you even greater. You have shown me the way of love. Help me to walk this way throughout my sojourn on this earth. May the rule of love be the rule of the day—and may it extend not only to my brothers and sisters, but to all your creation.

Reflection Questions

1. How do you understand your relationship to the world?
2. Do you think of the world as part of God's creation and

do you see yourself as part of this great creation? Or is the world something that has always been and always will be?

3. Do you feel any responsibility toward the world in which we live? Do you feel connected with it? Do you think of it as being tied up with your destiny?

4. Do you reflect on the natural world around you? Pray about it? Are you aware of the way you interact with it? Do you care for it or abuse it? Do you tend it or exhaust it? Do you love it or hate it? Are you indifferent toward it? Overwhelmed by it?

5. What attitudes of yours about God's creation need changing? What behaviors?

6. How have you contributed to or participated in the environment's destruction? Have you asked God's forgiveness for what you have done? What practical steps have you taken to improve it? If none, what could be done?

Exercise

Take a walk in nature—possibly on a mountain path, in a meadow or field, or in a nearby park. Look around you. Notice the great variety of living and nonliving things. Thank God for the many gifts with which you have been blessed. Thank God for the world you are living in and the way you are situated in it. Thank God from the bottom of your heart for the glory of creation—and then imagine. Imagine it was all gone, damaged beyond repair. Imagine the world lost— lost on account of human carelessness. Imagine that the loss was created by your own carelessness. Ask God's forgiveness for your participation in the destruction of the environment. Ask God to help you make amends.

Soliloquy Prayer 3
Examining My Heart

Introduction

Part of the reason why many of us do not feel at home in the world is our own failure to feel at home with ourselves. We live life on the surface and rarely, if ever, take the time to delve beneath the level of appearances. As a result, we distance ourselves from our own hearts and never get to know ourselves as we really are.

The next soliloquy tries to peel away the various levels of self-deception that have gotten in the way of our relationship to God. It looks at the subtle ways we have tried to control God and to fashion him in our own image and likeness. It also brings to the fore what is important in sharing and maintaining a close intimate relationship with him. We cannot relate to God from the heart if we ourselves do not understand our heart's own movement in our lives. If we do not examine our hearts and bare them open out of love and concern for others, we will continue to remain strangers to ourselves, to others, to God, and to the world.

Psalm

For I know my offense;
  my sin is always before me.
Against you only have I sinned;
  I have done such evil in your sight
That you are just in your sentence,
  blameless when you condemn.

True, I was born guilty,
   a sinner, even as my mother conceived me.
Still, you insist on sincerity of heart;
   in my inmost being teach me wisdom.

Psalm 51:5–8

Meditation

But against all these annoyances, and all others that may befall, use this remedy: take Jesus in your mind, and do not be angry with them; do not linger with them, but think of your lesson—that you are nothing, you have nothing, you cannot lose any earthly goods, and you desire nothing but the love of Jesus—and keep on your way to Jerusalem, with your occupation.

Walter Hilton, *The Scale of Perfection*, 2.22

Soliloquy Prayer

Lord, I feel as though I have forgotten how to speak to you. I do not know what to say. My tongue gets all tied up and nothing comes out. I look at what I have written and am embarrassed by its stiff formality. That is not the way I was taught to speak to you. I was given the faith of a little child and have somehow lost it. I approach you with all the sophistication that my deep interior sense tells me is not how you want me to relate to you. It is as though I put on a mask whenever I talk to you. I feel as though I am acting, as though I am not really revealing my deepest, truest self to you.

Why is that, Lord? Is there something about my true self, my inner self, that I am ashamed of or afraid to look at? I know that I do not have to put on a show whenever I turn to you. I know that you already know me as I am, with all my human frailties. I know all of this, and yet for some reason I still find it difficult to talk to you. I feel as though my words need to be precise, that you will not listen to me if they are not just right. Worse still, I act out on the basis of these feelings, even though I know that they are immature.

The thought has just occurred to me that such prayers may be a subtle attempt on my part to control you. I remember how, years and years ago, I used to cross myself over and over and over again, thinking that, if I got it just right, you would hear my prayer and answer my petition. How childish I was and, to a large extent, still am. Is not all this formality nothing more than a more complex and sophisticated way of getting you to hear me so that I will get the things I want from you? Now I see it. Some parts of me have never changed. I act as though I have, but deep inside I know and you know that I have not.

It is not easy to write what I have just written, Lord. I now see that if I am to have a strong relationship with you, I must take off all the masks and self-deceptions that I have convinced myself that I could not do without. I have to strip myself of these useless accessories and get back to the basics. Help me to do so, Lord. I have forgotten the meaning of simplicity. I no longer know what it means to trust in you in the concrete, day-to-day circumstances of my life. I have allowed *my* will, *my* expectations, *my own* personal agenda to get in the way. Help me, Lord. Only you can free me of the bonds of sophistication that make me want to be more than I really am. Help me to see myself as you see me. Burn that image deep within my heart and never let me forget it.

I wish, Lord, that I could always be aware of your presence in my heart. I wish I could live out of that awareness and be led at each moment of my life by your gentle promptings. I wish I could follow your lead at each passing moment of my life. One day I hope to be able to do so. One day I hope to be completely converted over to living a life fully and completely turned over to you. I hope that this will come to pass, and I am able to hope only because I believe that you can accomplish such great things in me. Only you can make me holy, only you can bring me further along the road of sanctity.

In the meantime, I will continue to stumble along, turning left when I should be going right; stepping up when I should be stepping down. I will continue to lose sight of you during the day and look back over the day disappointed that I was unable to share more of my life than what I did. Still, in all of my indifference and lack of attention, I thank you, Lord, that you can make all situations work out for good. I am grateful that my destiny does not lie in my hands alone, but in yours as well, and that you will not refuse my meager efforts to involve you in my life. I am grateful, Lord, that you look into my heart and patiently allow the wheat to grow together with the weeds. In your own due time, you will harvest them, sift them, and either thrash them or burn them.

Help me, Lord, not to be impatient with myself. Help me to think of myself as you think of me. Help me to enjoy your utter acceptance of me, as I am, with all of my faults and failings. Help me to accept myself as you accept me. Help me to acknowledge those areas in my life where I need to grow and to remember that I can do nothing good apart from you, that only you can bring about my complete and total conversion. Help me to ask for the things I truly need and not simply those things that will make my life easier or more convenient. Help me to trust you more and more with each new day.

It seems as though I am always asking you for help, Lord. I have no shame on that account. I ask and will continue to ask. Sometimes I feel that all I can do is ask. As a matter of fact, it is usually when I stop asking that I get into trouble by thinking I can handle things on my own. Such an attitude is completely contrary to your will for me. I know that you want to be involved in my affairs. I know that you want to be invited to participate in my daily activities. I know that you want to be present in the nitty gritty circumstances of my life.

Lord, I remember the closeness and intimacy that I felt when I first found you, so long, long ago. It was a special time of grace, a time when I experienced your nearness in almost everything I did, in the difficult tasks that you placed before me, but also in the joy of companionship that you gave me in my close friends and fellow travelers in faith. Lord, I remember those times with a special fondness. I look back to them, and realize how important a part they played in my life. I am grateful for your giving me such moments of intimacy. I can look back to them and remember that you have promised to be with me and to never leave me.

Lord, it has been so long since I have had that unique sense of your presence in my heart. And, yet, I have continued to believe despite the times when you seemed so very absent in my life. I have continued to turn to you and to ask your help, despite the very strong tendencies in me to want to step out on my own, without you. Lord, I have been strongly tempted to turn my back on you, to stop believing in you and to stop searching for you in the events of my life. But how could I ever do such things? How could I stop searching for you, stop looking for you, stop believing in you? You are all I have, and all I ever want. You are the center of my life, the reason for everything I do. To turn away from you would be to deny my own existence. To stop believing in you would deal a fatal blow to my own sense of life and selfhood.

Dear Lord, I guess I am more firmly rooted in you than I had imagined. It has gotten to a point where I cannot imagine not believing in you anymore. You have become more important to me than all else. I could not live without believing in you, and I would like to think that I would be willing to die for you. But, if all this is true Lord, and not just more of the same empty words that I have been using to deceive myself, tell me, why is it that I seem to have become so lacking in affection and enthusiasm in the things I do for you? Why have I become so lukewarm in my beliefs and convictions? Why do I approach each day with an expectation of boredom rather than one of risk and adventure?

I wish I could recapture, Lord, some of my past enthusiasm and focus all of that energy on something that would cry out and sing to all the world of your love for us. I wish I could be so much alive with my love for you that nothing else would matter but bringing you into the lives of others. But, Lord, I realize that such dreams would be fruitless if I did not succeed in bringing you into my own life more deeply and fully. And, even that, I now realize would be fruitless if I tried to force your hand and do it all on my own.

So I humbly ask you, Lord, please come to me, heal me, convert me, help me to turn my entire life over to you. Help me to keep my feet firmly planted on the ground, but my eyes always focused on the great love you have shown to me and to all the other brothers and sisters with whom I share this planet. You alone are my hope. Without you I can do nothing. With you all things are possible.

Reflection Questions

1. Do you ever feel as if you are putting on a mask when you talk to God? If so, what kind of mask is it? Have you ever taken it off? What would happen if you did?
2. Are you trying to hide anything from God? Do you ever feel as if you are trying to manipulate God? Do you ever feel as though you are just giving God "lip service"?
3. What do you really want to say to God? Why don't you say it? What do you think God really wants to say to you?

4. Was there ever a time in your life when you felt particularly close to God? What was it like? What is God trying to say to you now?
5. What does God see in you? What do you see in yourself?
6. Is there anything in your life you would like to change? Have you been able to change it? If not, why not? Do you think God has the power to change it? Do you believe God wants to? Do you believe God will change it?

Exercise

Look at yourself in the mirror. Stare into your eyes. Try to hold the gaze for a few minutes. Smile at yourself. Frown. Pout. Show anger. Distress. Fear. Make faces at yourself, whatever kind you like. Do you like your physical appearance? What do you like about it? What don't you like about it? What would you change if you could? Now close your eyes. Pretend you have been dreaming and that you have now just awakened. Quiet yourself. Look inside yourself. Try to imagine yourself as God sees you. What do you see? What does God see? Now speak to God—from your heart. Say whatever comes to mind. Don't try to pretend. Don't put on a mask. Just talk to God. Let your innermost thoughts rise to the surface. Share them with God.

Soliloquy Prayer 4

The Word Made Flesh

Introduction

Jesus was first and foremost a man of heart, someone who revealed to us the extent of God's love for us. He entered our world, gave of himself completely, and became our nourishment and source of hope. He was a man truly at home with himself and with "Abba," his Father in heaven. Our next soliloquy seeks to understand what it means for us to have Emmanuel, "God with us," in our midst. It acknowledges the problems many of us have with the doctrine of the Incarnation, admits them humbly to God, and asks for help in overcoming them. At the same time, it marvels at the great power of love that Jesus unleashed in the world when he taught his followers to talk to God on such intimate terms and to bring to him our deepest hopes and aspirations. "God became human so that we might become divine." Because of Jesus, God is not far from us, but close to us. He continues to come to us even today to show us the way to the Father.

Psalm

The Lord swore an oath to David,
a pledge never to be broken:
"Your own offspring
I will set upon your throne.
If your sons observe my covenant,
the laws I shall teach them,

Their sons, in turn, shall sit
forever on your throne."
Yes, the LORD *has chosen Zion;*
desired it for a dwelling.

Psalm 132:11–13

Meditation

I saw God was God, and man was man; and then it did
not astonish me that God was God, and that man was
man. Then I saw God was Man, and I saw man was
conformed to God. Then it did not astonish me that
man was blissful with God.

Hadewijch, *Letters*, 28.231

Soliloquy Prayer

It is beyond me how something infinite could become finite, how divinity could pour itself into human flesh. What, O Lord, could you possibly gain from such an action? What would you accomplish that you could not achieve otherwise? Why go to so much trouble? I do not understand it. I cannot fathom it; it seems so absurd, almost childish.

I agree that this is not a very good attitude to have toward a basic truth of my faith, but I cannot do otherwise. I am only being honest. The real question in my mind is why I feel this way. Where do such doubts and uncertainties come from? Why are they there? Why do I find them so unsettling? Here, too, I do not know how to respond. Here, too, I am uncertain—and probably will be for a long time to come.

My only solace is that faith does not require and, in fact, precludes absolute certainty. You ask me not to be certain, Lord, but only to trust you and believe in you. This simple acceptance brings with it a very different kind of understanding, one that offers an intimate, living contact with you.

I wish I could probe your mind, Lord, and know all of your reasons for becoming human as you did. These reasons are veiled in mystery to me.

Lord, do not allow my desire for certainty to get in the way of my embracing your coming as man with all my heart, mind, and strength. When I look back, I see that there were times in my life when I gave only a very weak and tacit assent to you, so much so that my faith had very little effect on my outlook on the world, and even less on the way I lived my life. I may have said that I believed it, but I really did not.

To me, the doctrine of your Incarnation seemed to me to be nothing but a stale expression of a bygone era, one that made no sense to someone trying to make it in the modern world. I thought of it as a childish belief, a remnant of my innocent, unsophisticated past of which I was more embarrassed than proud. This belief was a relic of my past, but one I preferred to hide from view and not share with anyone.

Even today, there is a part of me that is still embarrassed by my belief in your Incarnation. This self-consciousness is difficult to explain. I have committed myself to you and have dedicated my entire life to you. I want to follow you with all of my might. I want to give you everything I have. And, yet, deep within me there is something that holds me back.

There are voices inside telling me that I am wasting my time, that my faith is nothing but wishful thinking, that my faith cannot withstand intense intellectual scrutiny. I struggle with these voices, Lord, I do not want to give in to them, but sometimes I feel as though I am fighting a losing battle. So help me, Lord, help me.

I believe that you have entered my world, that you gave yourself completely, to the point of dying for me, that you became my food, my nourishment, and, most of all, my source of hope. I believe these things, Lord, but I want to believe them so much more intensely.

I want those doubting voices to grow still. I want to speak about you with conviction. I want to be willing to share your love for me with others, without feeling inhibited, without feeling embarrassed about sharing the most important aspects of my life.

There is one thing I am certain of. I can speak to you on such intimate terms only because you entered my world. I can reveal myself to you in this way only because you revealed yourself to me in the form of a weak and vulnerable child.

You know what it is like to be human, Lord. You know the feeling from the inside out. You know how I feel. You know the joy of friendship and human companionship, as well as what it is like to cry, to feel the pain of loss, to be taken advantage of, and to suffer evil at the hands of another. You became human, Lord, out of love for me. You wanted to be with me, to live with me, to experience life through my eyes so that you could love me even more.

Lord, thank you, for coming to me so that I could speak to you on such intimate terms. It means everything to me; I do not know what I would do without it. But, even here, the voices give me little time for rest. They laugh at me and mock me, telling me that I am only talking to myself, that my prayers are nothing more than a ceaseless and inefficacious monologue to an imaginary friend, a mere figment of my imagination. Lord, this is the struggle I go through. Some days are worse than others, to be sure, but I manage to survive. I only wish I could be rid of these doubts, that they would no longer hound me and affect my outlook on life.

The problem is, I do not have complete control over these feelings. They do not command me; I have passed that stage long ago—and never want to return to it. But they are still a nuisance. They make me feel like a halfhearted follower, as though I was holding something back.

I am not controlled by these feelings, Lord, but they *do* get in the way. I do not know what else to do to rid myself of them except simply to give them to you. And that is what I am doing. Help me to turn these doubts over to you, Lord. Help me to fix my gaze on you at all times. Help me to see your becoming man as a great invitation to turn to you at any time, to share with you my most intimate cares and concerns. Without your help, I will sooner or later give in to these shadowy voices and no longer turn to you in time of need.

Lord, thank you for understanding my situation and for knowing how to help me and what to provide for me at each moment. Thank you for all that you have given me, Lord, especially for entering this world of mine and for experiencing my problems from within. Only because you have done this for me can I turn to you and reveal myself to you in such a deep, intimate way. I also see that you want me to act similarly, to strive to enter other's worlds so that your love for them can flow through me.

You ask me to join in your ongoing birth in the human heart. You, who are eternally begotten by the Father and who became one of us so long ago, now seek to be born in each and every human heart. Thank you for allowing me to join you in this great and wonderful work. Do not let me inhibit you, or get in the way, Lord. Help me, instead, to be a ready and transparent instrument of your love.

I love you, Lord; help me to love you more; help me to love others. Help me, most of all, to see you in the stranger, to find in his or her eyes your quiet presence waiting to be welcomed and made to feel at home. You entered this world a stranger, Lord. There was no room for you; no one wanted to take you in, so you had to suffer from the elements, with little to wear, and only the breath of the animals and the love of your parents to keep you warm.

Every time I close the door of my heart, I act in the very same way. Every time I turn my back on a neighbor, I shut you out. Every time I fail to see you in the eyes of a stranger, I leave you out in the cold. I have been cruel to you, Lord, terribly cruel. Forgive me; help me to put these times behind me. Help me to see your coming in every new and changing circumstance. Help me to welcome you in every person I meet. Help me to welcome you in my own heart.

Come to me, Lord. Do not let me be complacent. You came to this world so long ago, Lord—and never stopped coming. You are there beside me, in everything I do. If only I had but eyes to see. If only I could see you more clearly. If only I was utterly convinced of your presence within my heart.

Lord, you came to this world so long ago because you were in love with it. There is nothing you would not do for us—not even die for us. Lord, help me to be similarly in love with you.

Help me to give up everything in order to follow you without counting the consequences. I want to follow you, Lord. Where you go I want to go. Lead me, Lord, lead me.

Help me to know your will for me and to discern how best to implement it in my daily life. Give me the patience necessary to do what needs to be done, especially when the task seems difficult or beyond what I am capable of doing. I want only to do your will, Lord. I want you to become flesh in my life. I want to be filled with you, moved by you, and led by you at each moment of my life.

Reflection Questions

1. What do you think about the Christian belief of God becoming a human person? What do you feel about it? Does
   it make sense to you?
2. Are you embarrassed by this belief in God made man?
   Are you ashamed of it? Do you really believe it? Are you
   proud of it? What gets in the way of your belief? What
   helps it along?
3. Do you believe God has the power to enter our world? Do
   you believe that God has the power to enter *your* particular world? If so, what is God doing there? If God is not
   present in your world, why isn't he there?
4. Do you believe that Christ is present in others? Do you
   recognize him in your neighbors? In the stranger? In yourself?
5. Do you find it easy to talk to Jesus? Do you feel that he
   understands you, that he knows what you are feeling? That
   he has gone through what you are going through?
6. Do you want to be like Jesus? In what ways? How does
   his presence in your life change your view of God? Of the
   world? Of others? Of yourself?

Exercise

Find a quiet place where you can be alone. Listen to the silence around you. Listen to the stillness in your heart. Now
imagine that Jesus walks into the room and sits beside you.
What does he look like? Describe his features down to the
last detail. Then begin talking to him. Let him know what is
on your mind. Tell him your joys, as well as your difficulties.
Ask him to help you to understand him and to believe in him
more deeply and strongly. Ask him, especially, to enter into
the room of your heart.

Learning to Pray

Introduction

Jesus was also a man of prayer. He sought out the lonely places of Galilee and Judea not only to find respite from the crowds, but also to find a place where he could share his innermost thoughts and feelings with "Abba," his Father. Prayer for Jesus was a matter of the heart, an action which embraced all of who he was: his humanity as well as his divinity.

Jesus taught his disciples to pray with humility and complete trust, with open arms and steadfast honesty. No need was too small to bring to God: no petition would go unheard; no request, unanswered.

The next soliloquy looks at Jesus as a man of prayer and looks to what it means for the disciples he left behind. Jesus talked to God using the most intimate words possible and asked his disciples to do the same. Jesus' prayer went beyond words and probed the depths of God's Spirit that resided deep within his heart. Because of Jesus, we share in that same Spirit and are able to commune with "Abba," our Father, in much the same way. All we need to do is open our own hearts to Jesus and say with the same honest yearning of his disciples, "Lord, teach us to pray" (Lk 11:1).

Psalm

Out of the depths I cry to you, LORD;
   Lord, hear my cry!
May your ears be attentive
   to my cry for mercy.
If you, LORD, mark our sins,
   Lord, who can stand?
But with you is forgiveness,
   and so you are revered.

Psalm 130:1–4

Meditation

God gives us many things out of sheer generosity, without being asked. The reason why he wants to give us some things in response to our petition is that it is profitable for us to acquire a certain confidence in running to him and to recognize that he is the source of all that is good for us.

Thomas Aquinas, *Summa Theologiae*
II-II, 83, a. 2, ad 3m

Soliloquy Prayer

Prayer seemed to come so naturally to you, Lord. You had such an intimate relationship to God that you were able to call him "Abba," Father. This way of addressing God went against the currents of Jewish custom and challenged your hearers to reexamine the way in which they thought of God and their relationship to him.

But I am not one of your Jewish or even Gentile contemporaries of two thousand years ago. I live in a world whose culture in the last couple of hundred years has subjected religious faith to intense scrutiny. It is difficult for me to address God as Father when so many of my contemporaries make light of his involvement in the world and even his existence. How can I pray to him when so many of those around me do not believe in him or, at best, think of him as an impersonal, cosmic force?

It is much more difficult to pray now, Lord. I pray because I believe, but my belief has been constantly shaped and reshaped by my doubts. Perhaps it is all the stronger because of it. Perhaps not.

There has always been a cost of discipleship, Lord. The particulars of it may have changed down through the years, but it has always been there. Once the cost was martyrdom; at another time, desert asceticism; at still another, denial of self for the service of God's people. Now it is belief itself, a cost which has changed the entire landscape of how we pray.

I speak to you, Lord, with faith and with doubt. I speak to you, Lord, because I have nowhere else to turn. I speak to you because I cannot not believe, and I need some way to touch you, to make contact with you, to let you know that, despite what everyone says, I believe in you and have staked my entire life on you.

Still, Lord, I am not sure if I am praying as I should. I need your help. I say whatever comes to mind; that spontaneity is not the problem. But I sense there are other levels on which you want me to relate to you. I sense that my prayer to you must not only be verbal, but also silent and still, that I need to seek you in the quiet of my heart. I sense that my prayer must go on not only in the daylight of traditional Church forms and practices, but also in the darkness of what is yet to take shape and in the shadows of my own deep spiritual yearning and questioning. I sense, moreover, that my prayer is not so much something of my own making, but something that you make in me and of which I am nothing but a weak, fragile container.

I sense these things, Lord, but I am not sure if they are of you or of me. I sense they are of you, but another part of me says they are not. Others tell me they are of you; others, not. I am tired of all of this questioning, Lord. I am fed up with the constant examinations and scrutiny of my faith. I am weary of the effort and am looking for some place where my spirit can find rest. And so I ask you, Lord, teach me to pray. Help me to converse with you as you want me to. Left to my own efforts, I will be forever second-guessing myself. I cannot leave such an important task to my own fragile movements.

Lord, I do not expect some entirely new teaching from you. I know what you said when your disciples put that same question to you. I understand that the words of the Our Father provide me with more than sufficient insight about what to say, what to ask for, and why to do it. I see in that prayer an attempt on your part to share with your disciples something of the intimate life you shared with your Father.

I too want to share in this intimate life, Lord. I too want to be a disciple. I too want to learn how to pray. But I do not wish to know just the words. There is something else I want to learn.

The disciples already knew how to pray. That knowledge was something as deeply ingrained in the Jewish culture of their day as lack of prayer is ingrained in mine. They wanted to pray as *you* prayed. They wanted to be taught by you, as John taught his disciples. At that moment, your words were just a vehicle through which you disclosed to them your intimate life of prayer with the Father.

I wish I could have been there at that moment as you opened you arms to heaven and turned to the Father in their presence. It was not so much the words that you spoke but the intimate life with the Father that they were after and that I am after also. At that moment, Lord, I imagine that you opened up to the Father and prayed to him with your whole heart, your whole mind, your whole soul, and you revealed to your disciples a relationship which they too could have and enjoy—but for the asking.

This intimate sharing is what I too am asking for, Lord. I do not know what to do or how to do it. What do you suggest? How should I go about it? To whom can I turn? Perhaps I should just continue praying the words of the Our Father until they sink down and settle in. Perhaps I should say them, pray them, time and time again, until the words are so much a part of me that they accompany me in everything else I do. That may very well be the way to go.

I doubt, though, if repeating the words of the Our Father over and over again is the only way. While those words are and will always remain the model through which Christians are taught to speak with you, it is really the spirit in which they are said and the relationship behind them that is more important. I could conceivably pray those words all day, and to little effect, if I did not have that deep interior desire to commune with the Father as you did.

That spirit and sharing is why the request, "Lord, teach us to pray," is inseparable from the prayer itself. Without it, the words lack the context of the intense spiritual quest that each believer brings to his or her relationship to God. Without it, the words run the risk of becoming a mere perfunctory ritual.

How many times, Lord, have I mouthed the words of the Our Father without really praying them, without allowing my spirit, my mind, and my heart to really rise up within me and spill over into them as they left my lips? How often have I allowed my mind to wander as I recited those words as if they themselves were some kind of magical incantation?

Lord, I know that the words of the Our Father are not the prayer; they provide only the opportunity for the prayer to take place. The prayer itself is what went on between your Father and you as you recited the words. That relationship, that experience of communion is what you offered to your disciples and, through them, to every one of your followers down through the centuries. You offered that experience of relationship to them both individually and as a group, giving them the opportunity to commune with the Father as the unique persons they were, but also as members of your Body.

So, when I ask you to teach me how to pray, Lord, I am not asking for the words or even the right attitude I should have toward those words as I pray them. No, I am asking you to show me how I can turn all of my being, my spirit, mind, body, and soul over to you and, with you and the rest of the believing community, how I can experience that communion with the Father that you possess and want us so desperately to share. There is no need for more words, Lord. What you have already said is more than sufficient.

But, Lord, I ask you, please, teach me how to pray. By this I mean come to me, move me, inspire me, live in me, yes, even pray in me, for I am incapable of doing any of this on my own. I cannot even believe on my own. This is precisely why I ask you to come to me and show me the way to the Father.

Reflection Questions

1. Do you ever feel that words get in the way when you are trying to talk to God?
2. Do you ever wonder if God is really listening? Do you ever feel like you are only talking to yourself?
3. Do you ever feel as though you have forgotten how to pray and that you have to learn all over again?
4. Is prayer something you *do* or something done in you or for you? Something you do by yourself or with God?

5. What does your heart say when you talk to God? Do you expect an answer? If not, why not? How does God respond? What does God say to you?

6. Do you ever ask God to help you in your prayer? What kind of help do you ask of God? Is there any kind of help you would be afraid of asking for? If so, why?

Exercise

Say the Our Father slowly. Notice how it is divided into two parts: praise and petition. Also notice the kinds of petitions that are asked for: bread, forgiveness, guidance. Ask for help to praise God and to ask forgiveness of God. Now recite the words of the Our Father a second time. This time, *pray* the words—and mean them.

My Daily Work

Introduction

For some people, work is a type of prayer. For many others, however, it is a meaningless drudgery or, worse yet, an uncontrollable compulsion as harmful to their well-being as any destructive habit or chemical dependency. Our attitude toward work says a great deal about who we are and what we hold most important in life. Understanding the way we work and why we work can open a window for us into the deep, interior regions of our souls. Do we avoid work out of laziness? Do we use it to escape from life or as a means of avoiding our true responsibilities? Do we work too much? Too little? Do we know when to stop? Do we know how to relax? How to play? Do we offer our work to God?

Work is not an end in itself, but one of the primary ways we give honor and glory to God. The next soliloquy encourages us to take an honest look at the way we earn our living and to see what we can do to make it more and more centered on God.

Psalm

Unless the LORD build the house,
*   they labor in vain who build.*
Unless the LORD guard the city,
*   in vain does the guard keep watch.*
It is vain for you to rise early
*   and put off your rest at night,*

To that bread earned by hard toil—
all this God gives to his beloved in sleep.

Psalm 127:1–2

Meditation

Anyone working, you should know, ought to work not
so much for the satisfaction of his own needs by his ef-
forts as to fulfill the commandment of the Lord, who
said: "I was hungry and you gave me food."

Thinking of oneself only is absolutely forbidden in
these words: "Do not be anxious, saying 'What shall we
eat?' or 'What shall we drink?' or 'What shall we wear?'
The Gentiles seek all such things." The aim which ev-
eryone ought to have in working is to help the needy,
more than to provide for oneself.

Basil of Caesarea, *The Greater Rules*, 42

Soliloquy Prayer

Lord, I offer all my work this day to you. Help me to do it
well. Enable me to determine what needs to be done today
and what can and should be done tomorrow. Help me not to
overdo it. Help me to find the right balance in the day between work and rest. Do not let my relationships suffer on
account of my work. Help me to put all things in perspective
and to offer everything that happens to me this day for your
glory.

It is so difficult for me to do these things, Lord. So often
I find myself pushed by my work, pushed to the limit. It is as
though my work consumes me and has taken control of my
life. I have forgotten what it means to rest in your presence. I
always have to be doing things. I always need to be accom-
plishing something. And if I am not, I feel as though I am

wasting time and, even worse, my life. Help me, Lord, help me.

All I really want to do is use my talents in a way that will draw others more closely to you. Please, Lord, do not allow my work to get in the way of that. Help me to put it all in perspective. Give me the ability to discern the role my work has in your plan for me.

Sometimes I feel as though I am hiding behind my work, as though I am using it to hide from myself and others. I do not want this to happen, Lord, but I must admit that, at times, I have allowed this work obsession to overtake me. Lord, I do not want to be consumed by my work. I do not want it to take over my life so that I wind up not having any kind of a life to speak of. Help me to appreciate the people whom you have led into my life. Help me to see them as your gift to me, and do not allow me to take them for granted.

Lord, what is it about me that drives me to work beyond my limits. Why is it that I have consistently taken a time-efficient, pragmatic approach to the things I do? Part of it, I know, is that yearning for success that has been with me ever since I was a child. I always wanted to be appreciated, and I thought that doing my best would give me the respect and attention of others. I still act out of these and similar motivations. Help me to do my work competently, but do not let me get too anxious about the imperfections that are bound to creep in.

Help me, Lord, to let go of my work so that I can use it as a way of bringing attention to you and not to myself. Help me do this, Lord. It is what I wish; it is how I would like to live out the rest of my life.

What a strange position to be in, Lord. I want to give my life to you, and, yet, so much of my life is oriented around the work that I do. I receive a great deal of satisfaction from my work. I like what I do, and I think I do it well. But, because I want to do it even better, there is a tendency in me to want to spend more and more time on it.

This tendency is a natural one, since my work involves creativity, and creativity takes time and effort. It cannot be turned on and off at will and certainly does not happen overnight. I feel all right about all of this, Lord, because I have a sense that you want me to use my creativity to help others to come closer to you. But I also know that there are times when the best thing I can do for myself, for others, even for my work, is to let go of it and to turn my attention to other affairs.

I find letting go of my work difficult, at times. It is just so hard to relax and not to think of what I have to do. I get lost in what I am doing and find it so very difficult to break away. Help me, Lord, to know when I should let go of things and simply take a rest. Help me to place my work in your hands and allow you to guide it.

A huge part of my difficulty also comes from my impatience. There are so many things that I would like to do in my life, and I feel as though there is so little time left in which to accomplish these things. As a result, I find myself filling up each day with more and more requirements for things to do. After a while, I begin placing unreal expectations on myself. I find myself competing against time, trying to cram more and more into less and less space. In the long run, I end up overly tired and the quality of my work suffers.

Lord, help me to balance my day with the right mixture of work and rest. Help me to focus on the things that really matter in life. Help me to be satisfied with less. Help me to let go of any expectations that are not firmly rooted in your will for me.

It is not easy to let go, Lord. It is a scary feeling. So much of my life is focused on my work. Part of the reason for this focus is my desire to make a mark on the world. You would think I would have outgrown all this by now, but I have not. The world as I know it is passing away. Why is my making a mark on it so important to me? Why on earth should it matter so much to me? It does not make sense! It just does not make sense!

But when have my actions made perfect sense? I have thought about this for a long time, Lord. A long, long time. Much of my motivation clearly stems from a lack of faith. There is a part of me that still does not believe in you. That part is deeply rooted and tells me to make other plans just in case what I have staked my life on is not really true. I find myself holding back. I am afraid not to make a mark on the world, because if I do not and if what I believe is not true, then I will have lost everything.

I see, Lord, how little trust I place in you. I claim to have given up everything for you but, in point of fact, have really given up so very little. I hold back from you the things—such as my work—that are most precious to me. I refuse to let you have them. I wish I could, but I am afraid to. I do not seem to trust you enough, not quite enough. My faith is weak. I am weak. I need your help.

Lord, help me to see what I am doing. Inspire me to turn over everything to you. Help me to give up my desire to make a mark on the world. Help me to do my work not to gain honors and a reputation, but to help others to have a deeper experience of your love for them.

You have given me so many wonderful talents, Lord. Do not let me waste them. Help me to use them and develop them, yes, perfect them! But let me do this in union with you.

Help me to open up my life to you so that you will be present, yes, participating in everything I do. Help me to make you a partner in all the activities of my day. Help me to look upon my work only in terms of the people it will help to come closer to you.

It is, at times, so frustrating, Lord. Nothing I do seems to turn out right. I push myself too much and get ahead of myself. I find it difficult to live in the present and to let your words arise from the silence of my heart.

I do not want to wait for enlightenment from you. I want instant illumination. I want to be able to turn your inspiration on and off at will. I try to control you by my words and, in attempting to do so, betray the very work through which I seek to give you glory.

Lord, I am expressing these thoughts and feelings to you not to inform you (you already know me far better than I will ever know myself), or simply to enlist your help and support (which I certainly need), but to help me to confront myself. My work is too important a part of my life for me to allow it to get out of hand and take control of me.

I turn to you Lord, to help me get a larger perspective on my life. It is so easy to get lost in my daily routine and to lose sight of the whole purpose for my existence. I believe I have a purpose, Lord. Right now, I have only a vague idea of what it is, but I believe that you know and that, in time, you will reveal it to me. I believe this, Lord, I do believe it. But help me when moments of doubt besiege me and lay hold of me.

I need to rely on you if I am to fulfill my purpose in life. I need to rely on you even if I am to understand what that purpose is. And I need to rely on you in order to conform my work, indeed my entire life, according to that purpose.

Reflection Questions

1. How would you describe your attitude toward work? Do you work to live or live to work?
2. Do you control your work or are you controlled by it? Do you worry too much about it?

3. Does your work lie entirely in the secular sphere of your life or does it have any religious significance to it? Are you proud of your work? Do you see it as a noble and dignified task?
4. Do you offer your work up to God? Do you ask God for help in your work? Do you pray while you work? Do you pray in and through your work?
5. Are you able to let go of your work? Do you place it in God's hands?
6. What do you mean to accomplish by your work? Are you normally happy with what you have accomplished at the end of the day? If not, why not?

Exercise

When you get up each morning say this simple prayer: "Lord, I offer all my work this day for your honor and glory. Help me to do it well and for the right intentions. Do not let it get in the way of my relationship with you, with others, or myself. Help me to be conscious of you during the day. Help me not to forget the reasons for my work. Help me to place it all in your hands."

Soliloquy Prayer 7

Looking to Friends

Introduction

Ultimately our relationships are more important to us than what we do for a living. If you want to know what people are like, just look at the quality of their friendships. Do they have any close, intimate friends? Does they spend time with them? Do they share with them in depth about the things that really matter in life?

The way we relate to our friends will also tell us a great deal about how we relate to God. The person who makes no time for friends will simply have none. In the same way, the person who makes no time for God will never know God. The next soliloquy takes a look at the various kinds of friends we may or may not encounter during our sojourn through life and recognizes that all of them pale in comparison to the friendship we are called upon to share with God. It asks God's help in helping us to love the friends with which we have been blessed and asks God's pardon for whatever we may have done to hurt them.

Psalm

Continue your kindness toward your friends,
your just defense of the honest heart.
Do not let the foot of the proud overtake me,
nor the hand of the wicked disturb me.

There make the evildoers fall;
thrust them down, never to rise.

Psalm 36:11–13

Meditation

A friend praying to Christ on behalf of his friend, and
for his friend's sake desiring to be heard by Christ, di-
rects his attention with love and longing to Christ; then
it sometimes happens that quickly and imperceptibly the
one love passes over into the other, and coming, as it
were, into close contact with the sweetness of Christ him-
self, the friend begins to taste his sweetness and to expe-
rience his charm.

Aelred of Rievaulx, *Spiritual Friendship*, 3.133

Soliloquy Prayer

You have blessed me with many friends, Lord. My close friends
have been there for me in times of trouble and have shown
me the meaning of love. They have been a great joy to me,
and I am forever grateful for them.

Other friends have come in and out of my life. I may
have been close to them at one point in time, but then slowly
lost touch with them, usually—but not always—because of
the great physical distances between us. With some of these
friends, I have been able to pick up exactly where we left off;
time and distance did not take anything away from our relationship. With others, however, it soon became clear that we
had somehow drifted apart. We realized that we had lost something that could not be easily regained. At that moment, we
decided either to reestablish our friendship, or to let go of it
in gratitude for what we once had but no longer shared.

There is a part of me, Lord, that wants to use the word

"friend" very sparingly. Part of me wants to reserve that title only for that intimate circle of those I hold closest to my heart and use something like "acquaintance" for everyone else.

Another side of me, however, wants to extend the term "friendship" to all of the people in both classifications described above—and to many more categories as well. This part of me recognizes something of value in each of these relationships and wants to affirm the goodness of each without having to measure them against a model that few are able to live up to.

Despite such big ideas about universal friendship, at the present, Lord, I like to use this word "friendship" to describe my dearest and closest friends, as well as those who have played a significant role in my life, even if it has been for a very short time. Such people are more than just "acquaintances." It is important for me to say that, Lord.

Besides, who am I trying to fool? You, Lord, are my dearest and most cherished friend. All other friendships pale in comparison with the relationship that I have with you. You sought my friendship even before I was born, before I could walk, or talk, or even learned how to pray. We got to know each other, gradually, over a long period of time. You were with me, Lord, at every step of the way.

You were patient and never pushed me into anything I did not really want. You stayed with me and never left me. There is no one, absolutely no one, to whom I am closer. So when I call you "friend," I mean something very different from the way I use it with my other friends, even those closest to me.

So, Lord, what am I to do? Must I create a new word for this level of intimacy? Must I call you alone my "friend" and relegate all my other relationships to the unsatisfactory category of "acquaintances"? I will not do this, Lord, and I do not think you would want me to think or act in this way.

Lord, I have experienced many of the different types of friendship and am grateful for all of them. I say this because I see in all of them a faint reflection of my own relationship with you. Even though they may not be particularly conscious of it, all of my friends are members of your one great circle of friends. Some may be more intimate with you than others; some may find it difficult to relate to you; some may not even believe in you. Still, I believe that every genuine human friendship will, sooner or later, find its way to you. I believe this, Lord, from the bottom of my heart.

You called your closest disciples your friends, Lord (Jn 15:15). They, in turn, were asked to share that friendship with others. One way you ask us to lead others to you is by simply becoming their friends. Your ways are not our ways, Lord. Your Spirit moves where it wills. You draw others to you at your own pace and in your own time. Help me to place my relationships with others in your hands so that they may be drawn closer to you in friendship. Thank you for allowing me to carry you with me at all times. Thank you for allowing me to share you with others by simply being myself and by allowing my relationship with you to shine through my words and actions. I love you, Lord, I love you. I cannot help but feel that my friends are somehow affected by this love I have for you.

Help me to be honest in all my friendships. Lord, you were always honest with your disciples. You never allowed them to deceive themselves with inappropriate thoughts or illusions of grandeur. Help me to be honest with my friends and, please, help them to be honest with me. Do not allow me to take my friends for granted or deceive myself into thinking that they are something they are not and could never be. Help me, Lord, help me.

I want you to be the center of my life. I want to walk by your side in friendship, and I want others to know that you are there. Please, Lord, give me the strength to be your good friend. Give me the wisdom to know when to speak up and when to be quiet. Help me to be aware of anything that is wrong in my relationship with you. Help me to sense if anything has gone awry in my relationship with others.

Lord, I thank you for all the friends whom you have brought into my life. I pray for them now, Lord. I ask you to bless them, watch over them, and protect them.

I pray also for those friends whom I have lost during my journey through life. I am sorry if I had anything to do with this loss of friendship, especially if the pain was great and could have been avoided. I ask you to be with them as well, to watch over them, and protect them. One day I hope to meet each one of them again. One day, in your own good time, perhaps then, we will be able to look at our friendship and see what went wrong with it. Perhaps we will be able to forgive each other. Perhaps we will be grateful for what we had. Perhaps we will recognize that something still remains of our friendship. Who knows? Anything is possible.

Help me to let go of the people, Lord, who have let go of me. Help them to do the same. I am grateful for the role all of my friends—past, present, and future—have had in my life (or will have) and I ask you to be with them now and always.

You are so good to us, Lord. You are with us all of our lives and you are forever searching out our friendship. I am grateful for how you have led me, for all that you have taught me. I know that you have much more to teach me about my relationship to you and to others.

Lord, help me to be a true and faithful friend. Help me to see you in everyone I meet. Help me to share our friendship with others. Thank you for all you have done for me, Lord. Thank you for being a trusty and sturdy shelter. What more could I possibly ask for?

Reflection Questions

1. Are some of your friendships closer and more intimate than others?
2. Do you have any close friends? How did you get to know each other? What is it that is special in your relationship?
3. What is it that binds you and your close friends together? What makes them different from your other friends or from mere acquaintances?
4. Did you ever lose a close friend? What was it that went wrong in the relationship? Did you learn from it? Has it happened again?
5. Do you consider God a friend? A close friend? How do you relate to him? What is it that is special in your friendship? What is unique about it?
6. Are you afraid of losing your friendship with God? What could allow that happen? what could you do to prevent it?

Exercise

Write a letter to your closest friend. In it, tell him or her what that friendship means to you. Say things not just from the head, but especially the heart. Be as specific as possible. When you have finished writing it, read it several times.

Would you feel comfortable sending this letter to your friend? If so, send it. Would you feel comfortable reading this letter to your friend? If so, then read it. Would you rather express your feelings to your friend in some other way? If so, then how? Try to find an appropriate way of letting this friend know that you truly appreciate his or her friendship.

Guarding My Tongue

Introduction

One way we hurt our friends is by the unkind things we may say to them or about them. Speech is a great gift from God which can be used eloquently and for great good. Unfortunately, it can also be used as a means of poisoning our relationships with others and the atmosphere in which they are formed. Sins of the tongue number among the most hideous and difficult to root out of our lives. They can also fall among the most embarrassing. Once a harmful word is spoken, it can be taken back only with great difficulty. Its effects must be dealt with; its consequences lived with—for better or for worse.

The next soliloquy opens up this dark and murky side of human existence to God. It acknowledges the mistakes we have made in the past, humbly seeks forgiveness, and asks for help to steer the tongue aright. However we express them, our words can bring out the best or the worst in us. If we fail to place them under God's judicious scrutiny, they will one day come back to haunt us.

Psalm

I said, "I will watch my ways,
lest I sin with my tongue;
I will set a curb on my mouth."
Dumb and silent before the wicked,
I refrained from any speech.

47

But my sorrow increased;
my heart smoldered within me.
In my thoughts a fire blazed up,
and I broke into speech.

Psalm 39:2–4

Meditation

True simplicity is better than abundant talkativeness.
Holy inarticulateness is better than sinful eloquence. He
who, without being asked, often gives way to garrulous-
ness, is quickly condemned. Accustom your tongue, then,
to speak well. Precious is the tongue which knows only
how to form words concerning divine matters; holy is
the mouth from which heavenly speeches always come.

Alan of Lille, The Art of Preaching, 26

Soliloquy Prayer

I wish that I could go back over my life, Lord, and blot out
every hurtful word I have ever spoken. That erasing would
be a tall order to fill, since I have verbally abused others in
any number of ways.

That is not to say that I have never been the target of
similar or even worse verbal mistreatment. But my own mistreatment provides no excuse for my treatment of others. I
know I do wrong when I say something that cuts another
person down. The problem is I cannot always control myself,
or I realize what I have done after the fact, when it is too late
and the damage has already been done.

I need to be careful with my words, Lord. Through them,
I can comfort a weary heart or inflict untold amounts of pain.
The choice is mine. Once spoken, I cannot take them back—
not really. They go out from me and take on a separate life.

They can help others or haunt them; heal them or wound them; bring life to them or kill them.

I feel so embarrassed and sad when I think of the many times in my life that I have used my tongue against the purposes for which it was created. I wish I could change the way I use my words, Lord. I wish I could use them only to help others, and especially to help them draw closer to you. But I am so weak and thoughtless.

Harmful things come out of my mouth almost before I realize it. I talk about others unfairly behind their backs. I stretch the truth or sometimes even change it to fit my own needs. I will go to great lengths to cover up something that should be known but would embarrass me.

I need your help, Lord, in choosing my words. Help me to hold back and never say something clever or witty at the expense of another's dignity or self-esteem. Help me to put myself in their place, to treat them as I would want to be treated myself.

Help me to say things only to help and never to hurt. Help me to be kind to others by my words. Help me to give them the benefit of the doubt and help me not to retaliate when I find my reputation scorned or in some way diminished by another's unkindness to me.

I need your help, Lord, in so many ways. Left to my own puny resources I would continue to make a mess of my life and others' lives through the words I say. Help me to change the way I use words in my life. I have become so sensitive to the way I can hurt others through my words. I want to get even closer to you. I want to live in you and you in me. I want your words to be my words; my words to be your words.

I am not just saying this, Lord. I truly mean for your words to become my words and would like it to occur. I want to bring you to others. But how can I do that when my own tongue is used as an instrument to bring others down? How can I follow you when my words get in the way and prevent me from following even the simplest of your commands? How can I be Christ to others when others perceive me as someone who uses his words for his own benefit and at the expense of others?

Lord, I need you to change my life. I need you to tear out the old self and to help me put on the new one. I cannot do it alone. Without your help, I will never be able to rise above my petty weaknesses and evil inclinations. So help me, Lord, please help me.

It is not just my spoken words, Lord. Any external expression of my inner life can be thought of as a "word." Any gesture or deed, facial expression or sigh can be considered a "word," if it comes from within, and is in some way directed toward or is perceived by another. In this sense, my entire life, Lord, has been one long string of words—whether uttered through my voice, my face, my body, or my acts.

You see everything that goes on: the good, the bad, as well as the ugly. You see all that I direct toward you and toward others, but also those things which remain hidden, which I do all alone, in private, even those things of which I am only vaguely aware, my reflexes and gut reactions, my inner attitudes which come out in my intonations and the subtle movements of my body. All of these things can be thought of as "words," Lord, and it shows me how much I need your help.

If I can barely control my spoken words, how can I ever hope to control all the other inner or silent "words" which spill out of me at every moment of my life? What can I do to hold them in? How can I stop them before they do harm to others? Without your help, Lord, there is no way I can control my words.

But I am not so much looking for control, Lord, as an

inner transformation that will make control no longer necessary. My inability to restrain myself is nothing but a symptom of my own lack of inner peace, of the discord in my own heart that prevents me from being truly at rest in your Spirit. I do not so much want to contain my words, Lord, as to be healed inside so that there will be no need to hold back or to rein in what I say. I wish to be converted, Lord, in my heart.

Please change in me the selfishness that provides the interior conditions that enable my unkind external expressions. I want to be so close to you, so in tune with your Spirit, so much in harmony with your will, and with your Word that nothing I say will be misconstrued or thought of as being out of touch with your love.

I know this request for change is asking a lot, Lord, and it may very well be that, to arrive at this inner transformation, I will need a good deal of self-restraint to help me along. All I ask is that you help me walk this way of inner transformation.

Without you, I cannot discipline myself. Without you, I will not know what to do. I need your help to cooperate with your help. I need your help even to ask for your help. I need your help even to do that. Lord, help me. I lift myself up to you and humbly ask you to change me. Convert me, Lord, and I will be converted.

Lord, it is easy for me to say, even to write, that I want you to be the center of my life. It is much harder for me to live that out in practice, especially when things do not go my way. Words come easy; it is much more difficult to back up one's words with one's life. You backed up your words with your life, Lord, and, even though part of me resists, I know you are asking me to do the same.

Asking you to be the Lord of my life means giving up that part of my life that has become so precious to me and over which I still have a great deal of control, that is, my time. Backing up my words with my life means being willing to let go of my life and whatever controls I place on my time, and allowing you to work in my life in your own time, as you see fit, whenever and wherever that occurs.

You have a completely different outlook toward time, Lord. In your eyes, "one day is as a thousand years and a thousand years are as a single day" (2 Pet 3:8). Help me to let go of my life so that you can take it and transform it as you see fit. Help me to be patient with my own impatience and to be open to the movement of your Spirit in my life whenever it occurs.

Your words do not return in vain, Lord. Your word to me has been a promise to heal me and to effect in me a fundamental conversion of heart. Help me to trust in your promise. Help me to be aware of your presence in my life in all circumstances, in all the nitty gritty details of my daily existence.

Do not let me lose faith in your promises, but help me to be encouraged by your words and by the hope that one day I will see them fulfilled in my life. Change my words, Lord, into hymns of praise. Help me to seek and to speak your word for others before I replace them thoughtlessly with my own. Help me to seek your word for me and for others in the silence of my heart.

Reflection Questions

1. Are you a person of your word? Do you keep it when you give it to someone? Do you take it back easily?
2. What do your words mean to you? Are you aware of the power behind them? Do you use them to build others up? To tear them down?
3. Do you think before you speak? Do you reflect about what you are going to say?

4. Do you let your words fester inside of you? Do you bite back at others? Do you talk about them behind their backs? Do you say things about them that are not true?

5. Can you control what you say about others? If not, what do you think would help you?

6. Do you apologize after you hurt someone with your words? Do you try to make it up to them? Do you ask God for help? If not, why not?

Exercise

Try to remember the last time you said something harmful to another person or persons. What did you say? What was the context in which you said it? Did you mean it? Write down what you said. Look at it, each and every word. Apologize to that person or persons in your heart. Resolve to do so in person if you can. Now cross out the words with ink until you can no longer see them. Tear the paper up and throw it away. Think of a way in which you can make amends.

Taming My Emotions

Introduction

Our words not only convey our thoughts, but also our feelings. When these get out of hand, they can cause everything in our lives to go awry, especially our relationships. For this reason alone, it is important for us to understand why we feel the way we do. When we neglect the emotional side of our lives, we pay for it in a host of other ways. We become trapped in destructive habits, stuck in abusive relationships, and lost in a complicated maze of self-deceptions.

Only by sharing our feelings with others and trying to see them through someone else's eyes can we hope to tame them and allow them to speak to us. The next soliloquy seeks to do just that. It delves into the emotions and expresses them to God, the one person in our lives who is *sure* to understand them.

When we hold nothing back from God, we eventually come to see that he, all the while, has been holding nothing back from us. This knowledge deepens our sense of God's abiding presence in our lives and encourages us to risk sharing our feelings with still others.

Psalm

LORD, my God, I call out by day;
at night I cry aloud in your presence.
Let my prayer come before you;
incline your ear to my cry.

For my soul is filled with troubles;
    my life draws near to Sheol.
I am reckoned with those who
go down into the pit;
    I am weak, without strength.

Psalm 88:2–5

Meditation

O foolish humans, how can that which was made in the image and likeness of God exist without testing? For Man must be examined more than any other creature, and therefore he must be tested through every other creature.

Spirit is to be tested by spirit, flesh by flesh, earth by water, fire by cold, fight by resistance, good by evil, beauty by deformity, poverty by riches, sweetness by bitterness, health by sickness, long by short, hard by soft, height by depth, light by darkness, life by death, Paradise by punishments, the Heavenly Kingdom by Gehenna, earthly things and heavenly things by heavenly things. Hence Man is tested by every creature, in Paradise, on earth, in Hell; and then he is placed in Heaven. You see clearly only a few things among many that are hidden from your eyes. So why do you deride what is right, plain and just, and good among all good things in the sight of God? Why do you think these things unjust? God is just, but the human race is unjust in transgressing God's precepts when it claims to be wiser than God.

Hildegard of Bingen, *Scivias*, 1.2.29

Soliloquy Prayer

Some things are just plain difficult to talk about, Lord—to
you or to anyone. My emotions are one of them. I do not
really know why. Perhaps I am out of touch with them. Perhaps I feel embarrassed by them. Perhaps I was brought up,
educated from very early on not to let them show. Perhaps I
hold them in for fear of being hurt or, worse yet, laughed at.
Perhaps I think no one really cares about the way I feel. The
reason for my difficulty could be any one or any combination of these. I am not really sure. All I know is that it is
difficult to talk about my emotions.

The strange thing about this reticence is that you already know how I feel. What I would share would be nothing new to you. It is the act of sharing itself, of having to
confront you and look at you face to face that I cannot seem
to deal with—or, at least, not very well.

I know you know how I feel, but I cannot bring myself
to share it with you because I find it so difficult to show you
who I really am. Why is that, Lord? Why do I hold back? I
feel like a child who is afraid of facing his or her parents after
being discovered in some wrongdoing. Am I afraid of being
punished? Am I ashamed of the way I am? Is it because I do
not trust you enough? Is that why I hide from you? Is that it?

"Love has no room for fear; rather, perfect love casts
out all fear" (1 Jn 4:18). Despite my reservations, Lord, you
still tell me not to be afraid. You tell me that your love will
always be there for me and that nothing will ever take it away.
You love me unconditionally, Lord, but my love for you is so
weak, so meager, so conditional. I have such a long way to
go, and I sometimes wonder if I will ever make it.

Take the shallow love I offer you, Lord, and deepen it.
Settle yourself there, and help me to see your love grow in the
confines of my own impoverished circumstances. Help me to

delve into my emotions and confront them, whatever they are. Help me not to be ashamed of them or afraid of them, but to accept them and name them for what they are. Help me, Lord, to share my deepest thoughts and emotions with you, to love you with my whole heart, mind, soul, and strength.

Help me, Lord, to feel comfortable enough in my relationship with you that I will never again hesitate to turn to you with any thought, any feeling, any passion, whatever it may be. I love you, Lord. I want to love you more. I want to give you everything that I have, even my wild and unkempt emotions.

But just what are these emotions that I am so afraid to share with you? What is it that I am so embarrassed by and unwilling to admit? When I look at them with my mind, they really seem so petty and insignificant. But they are *my* feelings, *my* emotions, *my* passions, and, because they are *mine*, I need to own them, take responsibility for them, confess them—in the truest sense of the word.

So just what are these feelings, Lord? There is a long list, Lord. Some of them I am able to name, others I cannot. I need time to sort them out. I need to be patient with them, give them time. Eventually all these emotions—those I keep hidden and those that I do not even recognize as being there—will all rise to the surface.

There are, for example, my sexual feelings. I never was much good at acknowledging them. Sometimes they flare up and I do not know what to do with them. It is as though they have a life of their own and refuse to act the way I want them to. Part of my embarrassment has to do with this loss of control. I am embarrassed when I am overtaken by such feelings. I would rather ignore them and put them out of my mind any way I can rather than confront them and recognize them for what they are.

I am also worried about the melancholy which overtakes me from time to time and which sometimes borders on a light depression. Someone once told me that we get depressed because we are angry; angry, because we are hurt; hurt, because we do not get what we want. This explanation is true to my experience, at least up until the present moment. What is strange is that I can understand why I am depressed and yet not do much about it. It is a feeling of being trapped inside an emotion that I want to escape, but am powerless to do anything about it.

Besides melancholy, Lord, there is fear. This may be the strongest emotion in me. I am afraid of so many things. Sometimes I find myself making decisions out of my fear. I decide to do something or not do it, not because of its intrinsic worth, but because it involves the least amount of risk and the lowest level of fear. I do not like this side of me, Lord. I like to think of myself as bold and adventuresome, but really I am not. You know it; I know it. So who am I trying to fool?

I recognize, Lord, that feelings are neither good nor bad and that it is how I deal with them that counts. When I look at myself I see pretty much a mixed bag: sometimes I react to emotions well; sometimes very poorly. I wish I could say I have been able to integrate my feelings with the rest of my life, that head and heart were perfectly in tune. But that would be a lie. I have such a long way to go.

Lord, help me to deal with my feelings in a healthy and constructive way. Help me to understand them and react to them in a way that is appropriate to my situation in life. Help me to discern which feelings are in tune with your plan for me and which are not—and help me to act accordingly.

You know me, Lord. You have probed my heart. You understand my thoughts as well as my feelings. Help me to turn everything in my life over to you. Help me not to hold anything back from you. Help me to love others with a sincere and open heart. And let that heart be filled with a deep, passionate love for you.

Lord, I want you to be with me in everything I do. I want to think with you and feel with you. I ask you, please, to visit me and never leave me. Show me, Lord, how to bring my affections into all of my relationships. Help me to own my emotions and take responsibility for them. Help me to look to you at all times, in all situations, in each and every circumstance. And help me to remember that there is nothing about me that you do not already know.

Help me, Lord, to turn my entire life over to you. Help me to make you the Lord of my heart, as well as of my mind. Help me to bring you into the minds and affections of others. With you by my side, Lord, there is nothing I should fear. Help me to receive your love into my heart, Lord, and let that love flow over into all my affections, and all of my life.

Reflection Questions

1. Are you in touch with your feelings? Are you able to listen to them? Do you know what they are saying to you?
2. Can you share your feelings with others? With God? Do you feel embarrassed by them? Ashamed of them?
3. Can you control your emotions? Do they ever control you? Can you handle some better than others? Do they ever get out of hand? Does it happen often?
4. Do your feelings get in the way of your relationships with others? Do they contribute to them? Do they get in the way of your relationship with God? Do they contribute to it?
5. Do you have a more difficult time expressing some of your feelings than others? Which are the most difficult to share? With others? With God?
6. Do you hide your feelings from others? From yourself? From God?

Exercise

Use crayons and/or pencils to draw a picture of yourself when you are happy. On another sheet of paper draw another picture of yourself when you are sad. Do the same thing for when you are angry, upset, when your feelings are hurt, and so on. Draw as many pictures as you can. When you are finished, place the pictures on top of one another in a neat stack. Then throw the stack up in the air. Pick the pictures up off the floor and gather them in a neat stack once again. Throw them in the air again, this time higher. Notice the different arrangement of the pictures as you stack them. Throw them in the air again. Repeat the process until you get tired.

Soliloquy Prayer 10

Shouldering the Cross

Introduction

Sharing our lives with others means bearing the burden of their crosses. What happened to Jesus, the man of compassion par excellence, is evidence enough. Many people are threatened by those who sympathize with the plight of others and try to do something about it. Jesus' passion is a bold reminder of the cost of following one's convictions to the end.

Our own walk up the hill of Golgotha may not be as dramatic or as gripping as his, but it will be sure to engage us on every level and test us to the limits. The next soliloquy focuses on the meaning of Jesus' passion and death for our lives. It poses some painful questions about the dark side of human nature and has us imagine the part we ourselves might have played in his death, had the circumstances been different. It recognizes that Jesus' passion and death continues to be played out in the lives of his disciples and it values this experience for the underlying sense of meaning and purpose it brings to their lives—and to ours.

Psalm

Blessed be the Lord, *who did not leave us*
to be torn by their fangs.
We escaped with our lives
like a bird from the fowler's snare;
the snare was broken and we escaped.

61

Our help is the name of the Lord,
the maker of heaven and earth.

Psalm 124:6–8

Meditation

And here I saw a great unity between Christ and us; for
when he was in pain we were in pain, and all creatures
able to suffer pain suffered with him. And for those that
did not know him, their pain was that creation, sun,
and moon, ceased to serve men, and so they were all
abandoned in sorrow at that time. So those who loved
him suffered pain for their love, and those who did not
love him suffered pain because the comfort of creation
failed them.

At this time I wanted to look to the side of the cross,
but I did not dare, for I knew well that whilst I looked
at the cross I was secure and safe. Therefore I would
not agree to put my soul in danger, for apart from the
cross there was no safety, but only the horror of devils.

Julian of Norwich, *Showings* (Short text), 10

Soliloquy Prayer

Lord, I look at you on the cross and try to imagine the pain
you went through for the sake of the world. I look at you and
wonder what possibly could have motivated you to give such
a total gift of yourself and in such a bloody and horrible
manner. I look at you on the cross, Lord, and cannot take my
eyes off you.

Your death was as painful as any death can be. Your
executioners spared nothing when it came to inflicting such
horrible and inhuman torments upon you. Your body, your
mind, even your spirit were sorely tested—to the point of

breaking. You did not think you were up to it. You asked your Father to spare you this pain. You looked into your own heart and could already feel the isolation of one who was abandoned unto death.

Your pain was excruciating. Why? Why did you do it, Lord? I look at your tormented and bloodied corpus and cannot begin to fathom your reasons for expressing your love in this way. Surely, you could have found another way. Was all this pain necessary? Was all the blood and the gore absolutely necessary in order to draw us closer to you? You are God. With you all things are possible. Surely you could have found another way.

We are so brutal, Lord. Why do you put up with us the way you do? Down through the ages, we have committed murders and atrocities of every kind. We did so in the past. We did so at the time of your coming. We do so even today. Why do you put up with us?

Why is it that we are so slow to learn that violence and hatred corrode the heart? What is it that we must do so that your message of love will sink into our hearts and take root there—really take root?

It is always the same old story. Bloodshed, death, more death! The story has been repeating itself for centuries. Will we ever learn? Can we learn? Are we beyond all hope? Sometimes I feel this is so, Lord, and I give in to my deeper anxieties about the future of this world I was born into.

We have cast such a shadow of death over the world that it is hard to see through it. I get depressed and want to give up. At times, I nearly do. It is only when I look at you hanging on the cross that I realize that this is not the way you would want any of your followers to respond. Your story, Lord, has become our story. You died on the cross, but at that one decisive moment you also dealt a fatal blow to death, one from which it would never recover.

Lord, how can I enter more deeply into the meaning of your suffering and death? How can I understand it? What must I do to pattern my life after yours? Your cross is more than just a symbol; your passion, more than just another tragic story of needless death and destruction.

Your story, Lord, reaches out and touches the life of every person who has ever lived. By your suffering you touch something deep in every human heart. By your passion and death, you reveal to us the ground of our common humanity. By your wounds, you show us the cost of giving witness to what you believe in. You affirmed your deepest convictions with your life; you refused to compromise, refused to take the easy way. We who call ourselves your disciples must be prepared to do the same.

What a sad lot we who profess to be your followers are! The moment any difficulty or hardship appears on the horizon, we run away and abandon you just as your closest disciples did. How often have I denied you! How often have I refused to stand up for my convictions or pretended not to know you!

I have participated in your story for nearly all my life, but the role I have played is not one I am very proud of. I have mocked you and laughed at you; I have abandoned you and denied you; I have taunted you, condemned you to death, crucified you, and gambled for your garments. Not once did I show compassion for your suffering, Lord. I have let you down so often and in so many ways that turning from you has become a deeply ingrained habit. I barely know how to do otherwise.

Lord, I am sorry for all the blows I have dealt you. I am sorry for the less than honorable roles I have played in the ongoing narrative of your passion and death. I have played those roles so many times in my life that it would be difficult for me to change them. Yet that is what you ask of me. I know it is. You ask me to stay with you like the beloved disciple. To comfort you like the women of Jerusalem, to weep and mourn for you like your Mother, Mary, and the other women who stayed with you, there by your cross, to the very end.

Lord, I know I must change; I want to change; but I find it so difficult. I need your help to find a new place in your story. I need your help to follow you, to be a cherished disciple, to live my life in the way you want me to.

And then, Lord, the time will come when you will ask me to put aside my minor parts and to take on the major one. You will ask me not only to shoulder your cross, but also to play your part. You will ask me to participate in your passion, to make my suffering your suffering, my pain your pain.

To be honest, I do not know if I will ever be up to taking your place on the cross. I am so full of petty needs and my own private agenda. I do not know if I have it in me to step out of myself long enough to follow the way of the cross. I know I will stumble; I know I will fall. I wonder if I will have the strength to get up and carry on.

I have become so sophisticated, Lord, that I have forgotten how to experience the immediacy of your passion and death in my own life. I have placed a distance between your story and my own, between your sufferings on the cross and the trials and distress of my daily life. As a result, I have fallen out of touch with the symbol of the cross and have not yet found anything to put in its place. Help me, Lord, to reenter the mystery that your suffering has revealed to the human race. Help me to become immersed in that story in a way that will make a difference in my life and in the lives of others.

I sense that you have a plan for me, Lord, and in some way, that plan is tied up with making your passion and death more perceptible in the lives of the people I have been called on to serve. Help me to see you in all things, in all events, in all people. Help me to find the traces of your sufferings in my own meager trials. Help me to fix my eyes on you at all times. Help me to turn to you in times of need, especially in times of disillusionment and self-doubt.

Lord, help me to believe in you. Help me to believe in myself. Help me to carry my cross each day and to find in it a deeper experience of your love for me. Help me, Lord, in times of abandonment, when I feel all alone, deserted by others. Help me to see in those moments the comfort and encouragement that come from the knowledge that you have gone there before me, there, as in all things. Help me, Lord, to forgive those who have done me any harm and to offer them in that forgiveness the opportunity to be reconciled not only to me, but also to you and your Father. Help me, Lord, help me.

"Eloi, Eloi, lama sabachthani? My God, my God, why have you forsaken me?" (Ps 22:2). Lord, whenever I feel forsaken and alone, help me to look to your cross and find renewed strength and vigor. I know that your final words from the cross were not a cry of desperation, but a heartfelt prayer to the Father who has promised never to abandon his people in time of need. Your words reveal the deepest yearnings of the human heart which, in time of trial and distress, never ceases to long for the coming of the Lord.

Help me, Lord to remember your final words from the cross. May they never be far from my lips and may they forever remain imprinted in the depths of my heart. I look to your cross, O Lord, to find new meaning and purpose in my life. Help me to embrace the cross that you have prepared for me. Help me to embrace it, but also to look beyond it. For in looking at your cross and in longing to be your disciple, I realize that I belong with you. Wherever you go, there I long to be.

Reflection

1. Why did Jesus die on the cross? Do you believe that he died for you? Are you satisfied with the usual explanations?
2. How does your story connect with the story of his passion and death? Where would you place yourself in it? As one of his followers who ran away? Who betrayed him? Denied him? As one of those who wept for him? Are you one of his taunters? Tormentors? Persecutors?
3. Do you feel that you participate in the suffering of Jesus in any way?
4. Does his suffering on the cross somehow transcend time and space?
5. Does it have universal significance for humanity?
6. Is your pain and suffering somehow tied in with his? Is that the meaning of Jesus' suffering and death? Is that the ultimate meaning of your death?

Exercise

Read the account of Jesus' passion and death in Chapters 14 and 15 of Mark. Note the various characters who take part in the event: Judas, Peter, the other apostles, the chief priests and scribes, Pilate, Barabbas, Simon of Cyrene, the soldiers, the crowd, Joseph of Arimathea. Pick one particular scene: the betrayal, the denial, the jeering, the judgment, the torture, the burial. Close your eyes and try to visualize the scene. Put yourself in the scene. Play the part of a specific character (for example, Judas, Peter, Pilate). When you have finished, take out a sheet of paper and write down over and over: "Jesus' passion and death continues to this day. Jesus' passion and death continues to this day."

Soliloquy Prayer 11
Facing the Darkness

Introduction

We who shoulder the cross lift up our heads and peer into the darkness. Suffering is part and parcel of the human experience. We do not understand it, nor can we fathom its depths. It brings us face to face with the ultimate questions of life and of death. It forces us to look at our beliefs and to ask if they are really true and if we really believe them. Suffering also elicits from us any number of reactions: denial, repression, anger, guilt, resignation, acceptance, peace—and many more.

   The next soliloquy moves us further along the way of the cross. It asks us to get in touch with the many levels of suffering in our lives and to put to God all the heartrending questions that naturally rise within our hearts. Why did this have to happen to me? Why can't you stop it? Why can't you at least alleviate my pain? It then moves us to a deeper experience of the cross of Christ, reminding us that it is one day destined to become our own and that Jesus will be with us at our final hour to carry us beyond the pale of death.

Psalm

Foul and festering are my sores
   because of my folly.
I am stooped and deeply bowed;
   all day I go about in mourning.
My loins burn with fever;
   my flesh is afflicted.

I am numb and severely crushed;
    I wail with anguish of heart.
My Lord, my deepest yearning is before you;
    my groaning is not hidden from you.
My heart shudders, my strength forsakes me;
    the very light of my eyes has failed.

Psalm 38:6–11

Meditation

Lord, I make you a present of myself
I do not know what to do with myself.
Let me, then, Lord, make this exchange:
I will place this evil being into your hands.
You are the only one who can hide it in your
    goodness
and can so rule over me
that nothing will be seen of my own proper self.
On your part, you will grant your pure love,
which will extinguish all other loves in me
and will annihilate me and busy me so much
    with you
that I will have no time or place for anything or
    anyone else.

Catherine of Genoa, *The Spiritual Dialogue*, 2

Soliloquy Prayer

There are times in my life, Lord, when everything around me seems dark. Something awful happens that shakes up my world, and I do not understand why you allow it. A project fails. A good friend lets me down. Someone close to me dies. It could be almost anything.

I know that suffering is a part of life and that, sooner or

later, it will knock at everyone's door. But knowing that suffering will come does not ease the pain of its arrival—at least not in my case. The hardest part of facing suffering is the way these afflictions make me question some of my most basic beliefs.

I like to think of myself as a courageous person, but deep down inside I know the truth about myself. I do not deal well with tragedy, Lord. I react to it. I want to run away from it, pretend it is not there, or that it has not really taken place. I do not want the fragile bubble of my life to burst, and I do all within my power to insure that it does not.

Lord, when such misfortune arrives, as it has in the past and inevitably will in the future, my whole world collapses. I am thrown off balance. I do not know how to cope. I simply cannot accept the evil that has forced its way into my life. I feel as though I have a wound that will not heal, as if my nerves have been exposed to the raw air. The pain is heightened by the presence of threatening questions. "Why me, Lord? Why me? And why now? Why did this have to happen now?"

I ask these questions, Lord, because I have to. I cannot *not* ask them. They simply rise up within me. I ask them and know that I probably will not get an answer. And, I must admit, I sometimes wonder if even *you* have an answer.

In dark moments, I even wonder if there is any real point in asking. I wonder if you are really there, if you are really nothing more than a figment of my imagination, someone I had to create in order to cope with the tragedies that besiege me. That is what scares me, Lord. In moments of darkness I find my very faith in you is shaken. I feel as though I am looking down into a deep, bottomless pit. I address you as "Lord," yet wonder if the "Lord" I am addressing is really there.

Something within me shudders and my sweat pours

freely. Am I living an illusion? A lie? Is my faith just another, perhaps larger, imaginary bubble that will burst apart when that one final tragedy strikes? These are the kinds of doubts and anxieties that come over me when I find myself wandering in the darkness.

Sometimes these anxious voices are a strong influence on my thoughts and actions. At other times, they are softer and easier to cope with. But they are always there. They are always with me; there is no escaping them. But neither can they escape from you, Lord. Despite these anxieties and doubts that assail me in times of difficulty, despite my vast inadequacies and my weaknesses in faith, time and time again, I have still been led across the dark side of hope and found there a place where I can sense your elusive presence just within my grasp.

In the present world faith exists side by side with my anxiety and doubt. A certain knowledge of you, Lord, would lessen the significance of my walk of faith. It is difficult to believe in you, Lord—very difficult in this present day and age. Help me to turn to you in moments of doubt. Help me to remember your promises to me. Enable me to withstand the darkness and to wait quietly for the movement of your gentle, guiding hand.

I believe, Lord, because I must believe. I feel the deep anxiety of the world and wonder what could possibly alleviate it. I do not have any answers. I feel the pain when it comes. I feel the sadness, the loneliness, the depression. I feel the world crying at the death of so many innocent people. I sense the deep down groaning that every human spirit feels whenever violence overtakes the human heart and destroys some of the good that we have been trying to build.

I feel all of this sadness in my heart, Lord, and I find myself turning naturally to you. I almost feel as though I could not do otherwise, as when a child turns to a parent in time of need. I turn to you, and I cry to you, and I ask you why does it happen, not only once, but time and time again. I do not expect the answers. I do not expect all the suffering and pain to simply go away. I do not ask you to intervene in a mighty and powerful way so that the world would not have to go through what it does. What I do ask you is to help me carry on, to help me believe, to help me overcome my doubts, to help me find some bit of meaning in the dark loneliness that surrounds me.

Some people have told me, Lord, that you are nothing but a metaphor through which I am able to address my deepest yearnings and desires, that you are no more than the language that I, and others like me, have developed over the centuries to cope with our deep inner yearnings for transcendence. There once was a time when I thought that this must be so, that it could not be otherwise, that you are so closely tied to the words and expressions with which I address you that you have become virtually indistinguishable from them.

Lord, at one time, a long, long time ago, I believed that you were one with the words used to describe you—but I can hold this belief no more. I can believe it no more, because there is something in me that cannot accept it. It is *you* who revealed your Word to us by becoming one of us and showing us how to love. You are more than just the language I use to address you. You are more than just a sophisticated metaphor or a poetic expression. If that were all you were, then why would I bother? I place my faith not in words and the meaning and feelings they are able to convey, but in you who have revealed yourself to us and who are helping us find our way as we grope in the darkness.

Look at me, Lord, I am weak and frail. Nothing in me can withstand the dark forces that surround me and seek to destroy me. Death has fixed its mark upon my brow. I flee and try to hide, but I know I will not succeed. I turn my face and hide my tears from the crowd. I do not want others to know of my weakness. But you know, Lord. You are aware of everything that will happen to me. You know the day and the hour, the time and the place, the exact moment when tragedy will strike me down and humble me as it has done my parents and grandparents, and all of my ancestors.

You know my story, Lord. There are no surprises for you. You know the beginning, the middle, and the end of my tale of life. You know it all, Lord, and I know so very little. This is yet another reason why I must stay near to you. You know everything about my life: my past, my present, and my future. Only by staying close to you will I be able to find my destiny. Only by following the gentle lead of your hand will I be able to reach that place in the darkness which, for me, will turn into light—a faint light, to be sure, but a light nonetheless.

Lord, my only real comfort is my belief that you are present in the midst of my suffering; perhaps I am not fully aware of the way in which you are present in my suffering. Help me to hold on to this belief, Lord, that your are there in my sufferings. Do not allow this belief to slip away from me. Help me to retain it with my whole heart, mind, and soul. I cannot hold to this belief, Lord, without your help.

I cannot find real meaning in my life without you. I am unable to find it on my own. I must have recourse to you. Please help me to believe in the midst of my unbelief. Help me to find you in the midst of the darkness. Help me to see your light shining in the midst of all the shadows that surround me and the world in which I find myself. Please help me, Lord, help me.

I turn to you, Lord, in times of need, for I have nowhere else to turn. If you cannot help me in times of trouble, no one can. You alone can bring me hope in the midst of all my pain. To you I turn, Lord, because you have experienced the darkness firsthand. You embraced it by coming to us, by suffering for us, and by dying for us. Do not let me succumb to the darkness, neither that which surrounds me, nor that which pervades my innermost depths.

Come to me, Lord. Help me to cast out the surrounding darkness. Help me to find even the smallest sign of your presence in the circumstances of my life. There is where I must find you: not in the distant heavens, not in the depths of the oceans, not in distant lands, or atop tall mountains, but here, where I live, in this place and time, now, where I live and am experiencing difficulty. Here, Lord, is where I seek you. Come to me and help me to renew my faith and hope in you. Help me cling to you with passion, to proclaim you with zeal, to acclaim you with eloquence not only in times of prosperity, but especially in times of hardship.

Reflection Questions

1. Are you in touch with the suffering in your life? Do you share it with others? With God?

2. What was one of the most painful moments in your life? What was so painful about it? How did you react? Did you "clam up"? Avoid other people? Try to help them? Get depressed? Run away?

3. Do you see a reason for the suffering in your life? If so, what is it? If not, do you think there might be?

4. How do you deal with failure? With feelings of loss?

5. How do you deal with death? Do you ever think about the moment of your death?

6. Do you ever wonder when death will arrive? Have you ever wondered about what lies beyond it? Have you ever shared these thoughts and feelings with another? Have you ever shared them with God? If not, why not?

Exercise

Sit quietly in a room before a crucifix. Look at the tormented and bloodied corpus. Look at the crown of thorns, the scourge marks, the wounds in the hands, feet, and side. Look at them all good and hard. Then close your eyes. Imagine a cross with no one hanging from it. Look at it good and hard. Open your eyes. Look at the crucifix again. Examine Jesus' wounds again. Close your eyes a second time. This time imagine yourself hanging from the cross. Look at yourself good and hard. Open your eyes and look at the crucifix again and say, "I unite my sufferings with those of Jesus."

Soliloquy Prayer 12
Becoming Patient

Introduction

For most of us, sharing the sufferings of Christ in the daily circumstances of our lives means putting up with the little inconveniences that come our way. It means being able to suffer the difficulties of the present moment for the sake of those we love and have been called to serve. It means embracing the cross in the nitty gritty details of life and standing *with* rather than *against* those who have been forced to wait.

It is no mere coincidence that the words for "passion" and "patience" come from the same root Latin root (that is, *patior*). The two experiences are not dissimilar, but closely connected. In today's world, we share in the Lord's passion first and foremost by being men and women of patience. The next soliloquy takes up this claim by looking at the importance for our lives of this much overlooked virtue. It does so by examining some of our basic attitudes toward time, by expressing to God the difficulties we have living in the present moment, and asking for help in accepting the trials that come our way.

Psalm

I waited, waited for the LORD;
who bent down and heard my cry,
Drew me out of the pit of destruction,
out of the mud of the swamp,

Set my feet upon rock,
steadied my steps,
And put a new song in my mouth,
a hymn to our God.
Many shall look on in awe
and they shall trust in the LORD.

Psalm 40:2–4

Meditation

These three glorious virtues—patience, courage, and per-
severance—are rooted in true charity and have their place
at the very top of that tree of charity which in turn is
crowned with the light of most holy faith by which souls
run without darkness along the way of truth. They are
lifted high by holy desire, so nothing can hurt them—
neither the devil with his temptations (for he fears the
soul afire in the furnace of love), nor people's slanders
and assaults. Indeed, the world fears them even while it
persecutes them.

Catherine of Siena, *The Dialogue*, 77.

Soliloquy Prayer

Dear Lord, another thing on my mind lately is my inability to accept the frustrations and pains of the present moment. I begin each day with a huge list of things to do and get upset when circumstances interfere with my plans. I am such an impatient person. Most people would not be able to see it on the surface, because I hide it well. But my stomach tightens deep down inside whenever things do not go precisely the way I want them to.

I especially have a difficult time, Lord, accepting the possibility that other people's plans might interfere with my own.

I do not know what to do when the messiness of life intrudes on my neatly calculated idea of the way things should go. And so I get upset and take my anger out on others, myself, and sometimes even you.

I will give you a perfect example. I once had a particular work to do, but needed a number of things to happen before I could get started on it. These changes, however, depended not only on me, but also on the interest, circumstances, and time frame of a number of other people—and so I had to wait. I waited, waited, and waited, Lord. I waited for weeks, even months and, all during that time I got anxious, nervous, and exceedingly frustrated. I wanted to get started right away, yesterday if possible, yet things never seemed to get moving. As time went by, I felt as though I had wasted almost three whole months.

After what seemed to me to be an interminable wait, I then felt guilty about my impatience for a whole host of reasons: I did not foresee my predicament; I was unable to do anything about it; I was unable to wait in patience when I knew I should have. When the day came that I was finally able to begin my long-awaited task, I was so angry and frustrated that I could not act with an open and peaceful mind. I then had to wait even longer by letting things simmer down inside of me before I could act in an effective and appropriate way.

This example is just one of many, Lord. I could cite countless others. But why repeat myself? Other examples would be more of the same; they would all be characterized by my inability to deal with the frustrations of the present moment, by my growing anger and, at times, even by a depression that sets in when I am unable to use my time the way I want to use it.

Perhaps, though, these attitudes are part of my difficulty. Maybe my lack of patience stems from my attitude toward time and the presuppositions I make about my use of it. Perhaps I have become so pragmatic and task-oriented in my approach to life that I think of time more as something to be measured out and used than a mystery to exist in and be bathed in. In acting this way, I seek to control time, make it do my bidding, push it and squeeze it in order to get the most out of it.

Such an attitude, though, while productive and cost-efficient in many ways, prevents me from seeing the deeper, more important side of life. In seeking to control time, in trying to make it *mine* and only *mine*, I end up losing sight of its very meaning and reason for being.

I fail to see that time is not a commodity to be used and processed, but a mystery to behold and enter into. Much of my impatience, Lord, stems from the confusion I have about my relationship to time, and time's relationship to me. This confusion also enters into the way I relate to other people, to myself, and even to you.

What can I do to change these deeply ingrained attitudes about time, Lord? How can I let go of my anxieties and frustrations so that I can live in the present moment and find the peace for which I so deeply long? How can I let go of my plans without giving them up? How can I allow time to shape my projects instead of my usual approach of trying to make my projects change the shape of time?

Help me to let go, Lord. Help me, Lord, to be a patient person. Help me to understand what it means to suffer in the present moment, to wait on you as you are continually waiting for me. Help me to find you, Lord, in my waiting, especially in those periods of frustration and anxiety about the future. Help me to place my life in your hands and to allow for the realization of all my plans and projects to be accomplished, or not accomplished, in your due time.

I know myself, Lord, certainly not as well as you know

me, but I do know myself to some degree. Without your help, there is no way in the world that I can change my approach to the frustrations of the present moment. If you do not help me, I will continue to try to pack more and more into smaller and smaller periods of time. I will try to break time open, crush it, and, in the long run, pressure it and myself into doing more and more with less and less.

Lord, this way of dealing with time simply cannot continue. Sooner or later, my frustration will get out of control, and I will become the victim of my own inability to let go of my life and allow you to be the Lord of history, the Lord of my journey through time. It is not easy, Lord, to let go. But, by not letting go, I am, in effect, saying that I refuse to allow your plan for me to interfere with my plans for myself. I am telling you in a very sophisticated and subtle way that you may not enter into this part of my life, because I already know how I want it to turn out. In acting this self-absorbed way, I have become a disciple of yours in name only. I have held back from you huge areas of my life that are governed more by pragmatism and utility than the way of the cross.

Lord, I ask you, please, to help me change some of my most basic attitudes toward time. Help me to be more oriented to people rather than to projects. Help me to see how you entered the world of time not to accomplish great feats for the cultural advancement of the world, but simply to be with your people and to suffer with them the pains and struggles of the present moment.

Help me, Lord, to see myself in the light of your being. Help me not to be continually trying to escape this moment, but to live in it, with all its headaches and petty frustrations. Help me to live in it in such a way that it will give me a deeper awareness of your presence in my life and help me to shape my plans accordingly.

Thank you for your patience with me, Lord. I am a very

slow learner. Thank you for not turning away from me, but for taking the time to spend the time with me so that you could bring me along and teach me the ways of discipleship. I still have long way to go, Lord. I know it, and you know it. Help me not to be frustrated, but to be satisfied with whatever little steps I am able to make. One day I hope to live in a time that is all time: ever past, ever present, ever future. Help me to see a reflection of that time now, in the present moment, and to live my life accordingly.

But, Lord, I have mouthed this and similar prayers many times before. When I look back at it all, I see so little progress that I am now even frustrated by the feeling that my prayers are not being heard. Lord, I pray for patience and the ability to embrace the limitations of the present moment and to find your will for me there.

I do not feel as though I have changed. I still react strongly against the many inconveniences that come my way and make it that much more difficult for me to implement my plans. I say I want to let go, I ask for your help in letting go, but I still hold on. Nothing seems to change. Something in me refuses to open up to the movement of your grace. The end result is further frustration and an increased level of anxiety.

Why do I feel this way? What is it in me that keeps me from letting go? Why am I so obsessed with implementing my own plans beyond all else? Why do I hesitate so much to put my relationships with others, and especially with you, in the forefront of my life?

I need your help, Lord. I need you to help me trust you more. I need you to help me to embrace myself and accept myself as I am, rather than placing my self-worth in my accomplishments and in the things I do. Help me, Lord, to empty myself of all self-interest and to offer everything in my life to you. And help me, most of all, to be patient with my inability to grow.

I need you in my life, Lord, for so many obvious reasons. I need you to take an active role in my spiritual growth. Help me to entrust myself to you in this very personal matter. I am unable to change on my own. I am unable to trust you on my own. Without your help, I will continue to fill my days with useless and empty tasks that will bring no one closer to you and may even move them further away. Help me, Lord, help me.

Reflection Questions

1. Do you consider yourself to be a patient person? Do you deal well with interruptions?
2. Are you able to let go of your plans when something more urgent arises? Do you get angry when this happens?
3. Do you find yourself constantly trying to do more and more in less and less amounts of time? Are you able to let go? Do you try to control your life by controlling your time? What would happen if you loosened your grip a little? A lot?
4. Are you able to suffer the little inconveniences of the present moment? Do you know how to wait? Do you know how to listen?
5. Are you present to the other people in your life or are you constantly worrying about what has to be done next?
6. Are you present to God in the activities of the day? Are you aware of God's presence to you?

Exercise

Compose a short prayer that you can repeat again and again throughout the day, but especially when your patience is being tried. Something like, "Help me, Lord" or "Lord, I give this moment to you." It does not have to be very original, but it must ring true to you in both mind and heart. Write this prayer down on a card and place it on your desk where you can see it. Hang it on the wall if you can. Pray the prayer whenever you see it. Carry it with you during the day. Remember not only to say it, but to pray it often.

Growing Old

Introduction

Growing old calls for its own brand of patience. Time refuses to stand still and insists on taking its toll: our faces wrinkle; our hair turns gray; our bodies stoop over; our muscles lose their tone; our aches and pains increase. Since none of us can turn back the clock, it makes much more sense for us to befriend the aging process itself rather than trying to hide it, ignore it, or, worse yet, run away from it. We do this first and foremost by placing our trust in the Lord; that is, by recognizing that God's love for us is unconditional and not based on how strong we are or how we look. God loves us as we are, because we are, with no strings attached.

The next soliloquy asks us to look back on our lives and to imagine God's presence with us at every important juncture. It asks us to let go of whatever keeps us from growing old gracefully, and to turn to God for the courage and strength to accept the natural outcome of our lives. If God loves us and is always with us, there no need to fear whatever trials that lie ahead.

Psalm

God, you have taught me from my youth;
till this day I proclaim your wondrous deeds.
Now that I am old and gray,
do not forsake me, God,

That I may proclaim your might
*   to all generations yet to come,*
Your power and your justice, God,
*   to the highest heaven.*
You have done great things;
*   O God, who is your equal?*
You have sent me many bitter afflictions,
*   but once more revive me.*
From the watery depths of the earth
*   once more raise me up.*

Psalm 71:17–20

Meditation

There is not a person in this world who is not a voyager,
even if not all are anxious to return to the homeland.

In the course of this voyage the waves and the storms
make us seasick. But at least we are in the ship. Outside
the ship death would be inevitable. When one is swim-
ming among the breakers, however energetic one's arms
are, sooner or later one is defeated by the size of the
ocean and allows oneself to drown. To complete the
crossing, therefore, it is essential to remain in the ship,
to be supported by its planks.

The plank that supports our weakness is the cross of
Our Lord. He keeps us safe from the world that threat-
ens to drown us. We suffer because we are tossed about
by the waves, but the Lord himself supports us.

Augustine of Hippo, *Sermon*, 75.2–4

Soliloquy Prayer

As I get older, Lord, I look back at my life and see so many
wonderful things to be grateful for. I wish I could remember

everything that ever happened to me—the good, as well as the bad. You have been with me during all of those times. I only wish I could look back and see what I only vaguely sensed or was perhaps not even aware of at the time.

Thank you, Lord, for traveling with me through life. There have been so many changes, so many moves, so many turbulent moments, so many ups and downs. When I look back at it all, you have been the one and only constant in my life.

You were there at the moment of my birth, when I cried my first cry and was given to my mother to hold and my father to protect. You made them so proud when you entrusted me to them. They not only fed and clothed me, but they showered me with love and did everything they could to help me grow.

Thank you, Lord, for being there with them as they nurtured me and led me along. Thank you, also, for helping them to learn from their mistakes and for showing them how to say "I'm sorry." You were there, Lord, guiding them and teaching them how to guide me. For that I am ever grateful.

You were there, Lord, throughout all my childhood, as I was growing up and doing the normal things a youngster does. Thank you for giving me such a great imagination and for being there for me even when it got me into trouble. Thank you for never letting me get bored with life. There always was something else to do, another caper to solve, or another adventure to set out on.

During those years, I am sure I conjured up just about every conceivable situation a child my age could think of. I was excited by life and by the many possibilities before me. Thank you, Lord, for showing me the world through my childhood imaginings. I have carried all of them with me through the years and have become a better person for it.

You were also there, Lord, as I got older, when decisions

had to be made and the horizons of my world came much closer. Already in early adolescence and then in high school, I was faced with important choices that had great repercussions for the rest of my life. Thank you for guiding me in those decisions and for showing me the importance of following my heart. Thank you for taking me through the difficulties of my youth. You helped me not to give in to peer pressure. You taught me to respect myself and to treat others in the same way. You gave me the strength to admit when I was wrong and to ask for forgiveness from those I hurt.

You always were there for me, Lord. I may not have been aware of it at the time, but I know that my story would not have been the same without your quiet, gentle presence. You have had a great impact on my life. You were there guiding me throughout my college years, as I discerned my future career goals, as I decided what I wanted out of life, and what I wanted to become. Without you, my life would have been very different.

I have no regrets, Lord. You have led me to where I am, and I am happy that I followed. As I get older, I have come to appreciate more and more just how close you have been to me during my life and how much I have depended on you. You are largely responsible for the person I have become. You have been with me at every turn of my busy and eventful life. I ask you to help me to be more and more conscious of your presence in my life. Help me to see you in all people, in all events, in all circumstances.

Lord, help me to turn to you in times of need. Help me to open up my heart and to allow it to be filled with your gentleness and compassion. Give me wisdom, Lord, in these years of my middle age. Help me to learn from my past mistakes. Help me to look to the future with great hope and high expectations. Help me, Lord, to look forward even as I look back, and to always remember that, in whatever happens to me in life—both good and bad—you are never very far away.

There is so much to be grateful for, Lord. As I look back, everything seems to have passed by so quickly. I wish I could slow things down so that I could appreciate them and savor life all the more. I do not know how much more time I will have here, Lord, but I would like to use it to help others come to understand your presence in their lives. I would like to be able to help each person look back and say, "You were there, Lord, beside me all the time." Help me, Lord, to do this. Help me to help others see your footsteps in their past, in their present, and, yes, even in their future.

Help me to encourage people to continue their journey of faith. Help me to unravel the mystery of your presence in their lives so that they will be able to see your hand in the events of their day. You have done so much for me, Lord; I only wish that I could help you in what you do for others. I am sorry if I am presuming too much in such a request. It is only that I love you so much that I want not only to be with you, but also to do with you the things that you do for others.

I look ahead of me, Lord, and see myself years from now, an older person with little time left to continue on my earthly journey. As I look back, I wonder how I will feel, what I will think, what I will regret, what I will long for? Perhaps I should not get involved in needless speculation, for the future is still before me; and I may have a long way to go before my journey's end. Still, I cannot help but wonder; I cannot help but hope that, at the end of my life, I will look back and be filled with gratitude for all the opportunities I have been given to draw others closer to you.

We are on this earth for such a short time, Lord. We start out with so many possibilities, so many dreams, so many chances. And, then, little by little, the choices narrow; we are asked to select one path from many. We choose our way and sometimes wonder if we have made the right decision.

As human beings are wont to do, there is the usual amount of second-guessing; some of us regret our choices; others do not; still others feel a little of both. I wonder what the rest of my journey will bring me, Lord. I cannot say that I know for sure where I will be, what I will think, or what I will feel. In any case, I ask you now to help me in my journey.

Help me, Lord, as I get on in years. Help me to age gracefully, to continue to turn to you, to look for you in my successes, as well as in my failures. Help me, Lord, to look back with gratitude for all you have given me. Help me to accept my weaknesses. Help me to accept whatever physical or mental frailties that come my way. Help me at forty-five, at fifty-five, at sixty-five, at seventy-five, to give you full glory in all things.

I wish only to serve you, Lord. I wish only to be a reflection of your love for others. I want only to proclaim your greatness in my life in every thought, word, and action. You were there for me, Lord, at the beginning of my life. You have been there for me at every major step and turning point. Be there also at the end of my journey. And when I close my eyes to time and face the night before me, let the final words on my lips be "Help me, Lord, and praise you! You are Lord! You are Lord!"

Reflection Questions

1. Did you sense God's presence in your life as you were growing up and as you matured? Did you sense it at the time or only when looking back?

2. Were there any moments when you felt God's presence in a special way? Were there any moments when you felt God's absence?

3. Who are the people who most mediated God's presence to you? Your parents? A teacher? A friend?

4. How has your image of God changed through the years? What image do you have of God now? How can it be complemented? What needs to be added?

5. How has your relationship to God changed over the years? Has it weakened? Remained the same? Deepened? What could you do to make it stronger? What is God asking of you in this regard?

6. Do you share your relationship with God with others?

Exercise

Get out your photo albums and look at the pictures of yourself from childhood down through the present. Look at the many physical changes you have undergone in your life. Look at the other people in the pictures with you. How many do you still know? How many have you lost touch with? How many have died? Look at the photos again and picture Jesus beside you, growing up with you: as a child, an adolescent, young adult, even into your old age. Picture Jesus changing with you, as you are changing. Close the albums. Look around you. Imagine that Jesus is beside you right now this very moment. Say something to him. Be quiet and still. Imagine what he would say in return.

Soliloquy Prayer 14

Longing for Rest

Introduction

For most of us, it is very difficult to let go: of our worries and cares, of our progress at work, of our concerns about growing old, of our fear of death, of our need to be needed. The list can go on and on. The result of this difficulty is that we are always on the go, rushing from one task to the next until we collapse from exhaustion.

Slowing down does not come easy for us. We find it difficult to take time out simply to be ourselves and to relax. Perhaps this is so because we have tended to measure our self-worth by our ability to perform and by what and how much we can produce. Perhaps slowing down is so difficult because we never took the time to get to know ourselves in the first place and are willing to go to extremes to avoid doing so now. When taken to extremes, keeping busy can be just as much a means of escape as any destructive habit or chemical dependency—perhaps more. The next soliloquy helps us to take a look at our attitudes toward leisure and the difficult time we often have in giving up control and to letting God be God in our lives.

Psalm

My soul rests in God alone,
from whom comes my salvation.
God alone is my rock and salvation,
my secure height; I shall never fall.

My safety and glory are with God,
*   my strong rock and refuge.*
Trust God at all times, my people!
*   Pour out your hearts to God our refuge!*

Psalm 62:6–9

Meditation

A person should also rest upon and in him whom one intends and loves more than upon all the messengers he sends, namely his gifts. The soul should likewise rest in God above all the adornments and gifts which it might send through its own messengers. These messengers are intention, love, and desire, for they carry to God all our good works and virtues. Above all these things and above all multiplicity, the soul should rest in its Beloved.

John Ruusbroec, *The Spiritual Esposals*, 1.4.C

Soliloquy Prayer

When I take time off, Lord, I assert that I am not indispensable to the world. I show that I am not a slave to my work, that I can let go of it for the sake of other values. When I do so, I refresh myself, become mentally and physically renewed and am able to see my duties in a very different light. I am usually more creative, more efficient, even more patient, when I return to work after a time of recreation. When I take a rest from my work, I also have time to foster my close personal relationships with family and friends, and I give myself the opportunity to spend time alone with you.

One would think that with all of these important reasons, I would go out of my way to find rest and relaxation in my life. One would think that, with so much to gain and so little to lose, I would jump at every opportunity for rest that comes my way. One would think that I would carefully plan appropriate amounts of leisure into my daily, monthly, and yearly routines. One would think so, but I do not—or, at least, do not plan for leisure very well.

I wish I could do better at finding time to rest. It takes a lot effort for me to slow down, take it easy, and relax. I need to ready myself for it, prepare myself, get psyched up for it, and ease into it. Why am I this way? It is complicated, Lord, and I am not sure if I can explain it. I know it should not be complicated, but it is.

I look at my life and I see ample amounts of time set aside for what I call rest, but I wonder if I am really resting. It is difficult to do nothing when I have been trained all my life to accomplish nothing but highly specialized and well-defined tasks. And it is even harder to take whatever time I have put aside and to look upon it not as something to be used or capitalized on, but as a gift to be dispensed with as one pleases.

My difficulty, Lord, is in knowing what really pleases me. Often I am not fully sure what it is that gives me pleasure, and, at times, I am even confused by it. I often feel that the time I set aside for rest is wasted on needless distractions and peripheral secondary matters that do not really count.

When I ask myself who or what is most important to me in my life, my immediate response from both my head and my heart is *you*, Jesus Christ, my Lord and my God. I believe this, Lord, and I mean it. You are the most important person in my life. I cannot conceive of living without you. You are everything to me. Without you I am nothing. What bothers me, however, is that I can say that you are the most important person in my life, I can really mean it, and I still wind up spending so few of my leisure moments with you.

I realize that you are always with me and that you accompany me in everything I do. I know this and appreciate it, and I am grateful for your presence in my daily activities, especially the ones that are difficult to get through. But if you are as important to me as I say you are, I would want to spend more and more time alone with you, talking to you and listening to you in silence. It is not that I never do this, Lord. I do it, and I actually enjoy doing it. It is just that what I do seems so insignificant, so little, so small when I compare it to all that you have done for me. I want to be with you always, and I want you to be with me always. So help me, Lord, to give more and more of my time to you. Let that time be quality time, where you and I can meet, converse, and get on more intimate terms with each other.

I feel closest to you, Lord, when I am alone. That is the way I am. I cannot change the way I am, and I do not want to. I need time just to be by myself, time to do things that will refresh and nourish me. I need to rest my spirit, mind, and body with a whole host of renewing activities. I know this about myself, Lord, and you know it. I ask for your help to be at rest with myself so that I can find you within me.

But this request is not all that I ask, Lord. I also recognize the need in me to be with others. I am still very much a social being. I cannot change this side of my life any more than I change my private, solitary one. I could not change it even if I wanted to. That is simply the way it is.

You have led certain people into my life, Lord; they are there for a purpose. My family and closest friends are there for me in my time of need; I want to be there for them as well. Show me how to be present to them and to show them that I love them. Help me to find the right time, make the right gestures, say the right words that will express my love for them and show them that they are a significant part of my life.

These people are not in my life by accident, Lord, nor me in theirs. Our lives are closely intertwined; our destinies shared. Help me to be aware of this in my dealings with them. And help me to be generous with my time for them.

I also ask you, Lord, to help me to find the time to rest in you, not merely when I am alone, or with family and friends, but also in the larger communion of faith with all of its variety and degrees of incorporation. Beyond the Church, there is also my membership in the various levels of the human family: the local, national, international, and global communities. I have appreciated for a long time my need to join efforts to work in these arenas, but only recently have I seen the need to rest in them and celebrate with them.

It is in resting with another that we really come to know the other. This is true of God, of the individual, of family, of friends, of the Church, and of the whole human family. Help me, Lord, to use my leisure in such a way that will celebrate your presence in the human family on all of its various shapes and forms. Help me to relish the great gift you have bestowed upon me at all of these levels. Only in doing so will I ever come to know my brothers and sisters the way I should. Only in doing so will I understand the great gift I have received by being born into the human family.

And now, Lord, I come to the crux of the problem. I see the importance for celebration and rest with so many people and on so many levels that I find it difficult to find a proper balance of rest in my life that will truly be rest and not simply mindless activity or perfunctory action. Because it is impossible to do everything, it becomes necessary to choose—and to choose well.

I find a tension here, Lord. I want to rest with you, with myself, with my family, with my friends, with my Church, and with my community. I really do. But it seems I have been favoring some to the exclusion of others. It feels as though some of my genuine desires, my "pleasures," so to speak, are not being affirmed. I feel as though I have not struck a proper balance in my life, that my priorities are somewhat out of kilter. I do not really know what to do about it. Should I spend less time with you, when I already feel that it is not enough, in order to spend more of it with my friends? Should I spend more time with my family and less time with you or with my friends, or with my Church?

I put these questions to you, Lord, not because I expect an answer, but simply because I wish to share with you the type of things that go through my mind when I think about the approach I take to rest. Once again, the question of control comes in here. I am a little afraid of letting go completely. I still want to hold back. I am afraid of trusting you with my time. I am afraid of trusting you also with my leisure and time of rest. I am afraid of letting your hand guide the events of my day. I am afraid of losing control over my life and of ending my day with "loose ends," things I had not planned for or expected.

One day, I hope to be completely at rest with you, Lord. I know this time is a long way off, and I still have a long way to go. I know I have a lot to learn and countless miles to walk. Thank you for traveling them with me, Lord, and for guarding me every step of the way.

I ask you to help me to fix my eyes on you and your presence within me. I ask you to always keep that spark of hope alive in me so that I will never get discouraged. Help me to live by it, Lord, and to focus also on what is already present in those quiet moments of rest when, either alone, in the company of family, friends, or community, I sense your gentle presence around me. Thank you, Lord, for all your wonderful gifts, and, this day, I thank you for the wonderful gift of rest.

Reflection Questions

1. What is your attitude toward leisure? Do you seek it out as much as you can? Do you avoid it?

2. Do you think of leisure as a waste of time? Is it a good in itself? Or is its pragmatic value for better quality work uppermost in your mind?

3. How do you see the relationship between leisure and rest? Are you refreshed and rested from your leisure time? Or do you tire yourself out with too much activity?

4. Do you know how to rest? How to do nothing? How to let go of things for an hour? For a day?

5. Do you see any relationship between rest and God? Do God's rest and your rest have anything in common?

6. Do you know what it means to rest in God? Have you ever tried it? Would you know what to do or not do?

Exercise

Lie down on your bed. Close your eyes. Try to put everything out of your mind. Forget about all the things you have to do. Relax. Let your mind wander. Allow it to roam. Give yourself time to meditate. Take a deep breath in. Hold it for a few moments. Then let it out. Deep breathe that way for a few minutes. When you have finished treat yourself to a refreshing glass of ice-cold water. Then thank God for the gifts of rest and refreshment.

Living in Hope

Introduction

When we begin to allow God to be God in our lives, nothing is ever again the same. We gradually find a balance in our relationships with the world, with others, with ourselves, and especially with God. This balance stems from a deep sense of God's abiding presence in our lives and the hope of one day seeing him face to face. For the Christian, all else pales in comparison with this one basic hope in life. For this reason, everything in our lives should be oriented toward this one final goal.

The last soliloquy encourages us to look at these hopes and to express to God whatever difficulties we may have keeping them alive in our present circumstances. It looks especially to the Resurrection as the source of all Christian hope and encourages us to imagine how we would have reacted had we been chosen to be the first to experience Jesus in his transformed state. What we hope for, Jesus has already fully attained. In his risen state, we receive both a glimpse of our destiny as members of his Body and a deeper sense of what our final vision of God will be like.

Psalm

As the deer longs for streams of water,
so my soul longs for you, O God.
My being thirsts for God, the living God.
When can I go and see the face of God?

Why are you so downcast, my soul;
   Why do you groan within me?
Wait for God, whom I shall praise again,
   my savior and my God.

Psalm 42:2–3, 6

Meditation

To "seek the face of God" is to seek knowledge of him face to face, as Jacob saw him. It is of this knowledge the Apostle says: "Then I shall know as I am known; now we see a confused reflection in a mirror, but then we shall see face to face; we shall see him as he is." Always to seek God's face in this life by keeping the hands unstained and the heart clean is that piety which, as Job says, "is the worship of God." The man who lacks it "has received his soul in vain," that is to say, lives to no purpose or does not live at all.

William of St. Thierry, *The Golden Epistle*, 1.8

Soliloquy Prayer

I long to see you face to face, Lord. For the present, my knowledge of you is only fragmentary; I sense your nearness, but you also seem so very far away. I speak to you on intimate terms, but your words are too deep and silent for me to understand. I want to touch you, hold you, and be held by you, but you constantly elude my grasp. I want to see you now, all of you, not dimly as in a mirror, but immediately and directly—you looking at me, and me looking at you.

I wish I could have been among the first to see you in the glory of your Resurrection. What a moment it must have been! You appeared to them suddenly and out of nowhere.

They did not recognize you, at first, but soon made out the features of their crucified and now Risen Lord.

Why were they not able to recognize you right off? Because they were not expecting you? Out of surprise at what they had seen? Had your bodily appearance changed so drastically since the hour of your death? Were they experiencing something so new, so different, so utterly unique, that they needed time to calm down and adjust before they could acknowledge it as you? It could have been any one or any combination of such reasons, Lord. The important thing is that they recognized you as their Risen Lord and, in that moment, the course of their lives and, indeed, of all human history, would change forever.

I wonder how I would have reacted if I had been chosen to be among those earliest disciples of the Easter faith. What would I have seen? What would I have felt? What would my experience have been like? What conclusions would I have drawn? Where would I have seen you, Lord? At the tomb? In the upper room? In Galilee? On the road to Emmaus? I guess I will never know.

My knowledge of you, Lord, comes only through the eyes of faith. You ask me to believe the testimony of those who experienced you in your resurrected state. I do this willingly, Lord, although, it is more difficult than I would have thought—especially today. But I *do* believe the testimony of your disciples and, because of them, I believe in you. That is not to say that I do not have my doubts. My doubts are many, and I have struggled with them.

But my faith is all the stronger for it, at least I hope it is. My hope is to have as strong a faith in you as I possibly can. My hope, Lord, is to believe in you so deeply, so completely, so powerfully, that whatever gap there is between the faith of your earliest disciples and my own will one day dwindle down to nothing. I do so much want to be your disciple. I do so much want to follow you. I do so much want to see you face to face. This is my hope, Lord. I ask you to nurture it, to bring it along and, one day, to bring it to completion in you.

But what exactly do I mean by hope? How can I describe its significance for me? What would my life be like without it? I am not sure if I am able to answer such questions, Lord. They are difficult to respond to and even a bit overwhelming. All I can say is that I would be truly lost without you. You are my reason for being, my one and only hope. Without you, everything in my life would become stale and lose its meaning. If that happens, then where would I be?

My hope in you is not an intellectual process, but a deep yearning in my heart to be with you at all times. It is a recognition that there is more to you than my present experience of you, that my capacity for you is not-yet-filled and can even be deepened by your transforming grace. I look to you, Lord, and ask you to increase my capacity for hope so that my love for you will never be obstructed or contained. I love you, Lord; I believe in you, Lord; I hope in you, Lord. Let not me be put to shame. Bring this love to completion so that I may gaze on you and recognize you in every person I meet.

I look forward to the day when I will meet you face to face; I wonder what it will be like. Will I recognize you? Mistake you for someone else? Will I need time to adjust my eyes? Or will they already have been prepared by a lifetime of quiet expectation? Will the encounter be too much for me? Will it overwhelm me? Will it be completely different from anything I have ever experienced before? Or will it just be a continuation of what has gone before? Perhaps the answers can be found in one or all of the above.

My relationship with you, Lord, has never been static. It has been a living one, with all kinds of movement. I do expect the dynamic nature of our relationship not to cease, but to be transformed. It will become clearer, more in focus, more in touch, so much so that what went before will seem like a dream. I will have awakened to find you close by my side and deep within my heart. I will see you as I have never seen you before and, in the process, come to a deeper and more fruitful knowledge of myself.

I also wonder what will be asked of me once I reach the fulfillment of my deepest hope. What will you ask of me? What will you want me to do? How will I be asked to serve? What ways will you ask me to walk?

I do not think, Lord, that seeing you will mean the end of my journey. I cannot help but feel that you will have something else in store for me, some other mission, some other work. I cannot help but feel that you, who will have spent so much time bringing me along to such a deep, intimate relationship with you, will have something else in store for me, some other plan. I await that day, Lord. I look forward to it. I ask that you help me to be patient with myself. Help me to be patient with others. Help me to be patient with your plan for me in this life—and in the next.

Am I being too presumptuous, Lord? I hope not. I am only putting down how I would like to see things work out. I realize that I still have a very long way to go. And I know that, for all of my fervor, it is still very possible for me to turn away from you. Even though I cannot imagine what living without hope would be like, I know that I have the potential to betray you and lose all enthusiasm for you. I hope this never happens, Lord.

I hope that you will take me by the hand, Lord, and show me the way to you. Do not let me betray you, Lord. Do not allow me to lose hope. Do not let me fall away from you. Help me to overcome whatever doubts I may have. Help me to look to you at all times and help me to avoid placing too much hope in my own feeble powers to make it on my own.

I hope in you, Lord. All of my hope is in you. Without you

I have nothing. Without you I am lost. Lord, never allow me to separate myself from you. I want to follow you at all times. Wherever you want me to go, I will go. But I will be able to do so only if you help me. Help me, Lord. Help me never to lose sight of you. Help me to hope in you at all times.

I have so much to be grateful for, Lord. You have given me so many wonderful gifts and have showered me with so many blessings. I am grateful for all of them, and I am especially grateful for the gift of hope. Because of hope, I am able to look back to the testimony of your earliest disciples and sense the glory of the Resurrection and the new creation that is to come. Because of hope, I am able to live in the present moment and sense how, rooted by the past and looking to the future, hope already announces the presence of your kingdom in the hearts of your followers. Because of hope, I am able to peer into the future and look forward to the fulfillment of your promise, to the day when I, and all of your followers, will be able to see you as you are, in the glory of the new creation.

The hope that comes from you, Lord, gives me a sense of my place in time and in the universe. It enables me to live each day looking to the past with grateful remembrance, living in the present with joy in each created moment, and looking to the future with quiet anticipation. Hoping in you, Lord, gives purpose to my life and helps me to live it with zeal. Without it, time would overwhelm me, and I would lose my sense of place in the world. Without it, I would feel alone both in the universe and in the innermost reaches of my heart.

Help me, Lord. Help me to keep my hope in you alive. Help me to look to you always and to rely on you at each moment of my life. Help me, especially during difficult times, when I am tempted to doubt your presence in my life and when I lose sight of the meaning and purpose of things. Help me to hope in you. It is all I have. It is all that counts. Without it, I will not be able to continue. With it, I look forward to living out my life in joyful expectation of one day seeing you face to face, as I am and as you truly are.

Reflection Questions

1. Do you hope in the promise of Jesus' Resurrection?
2. Have you ever imagined being there with Mary Magdalene, with Peter, with the other apostles and disciples when they first experienced him? Did you ever wonder what it was like?
3. Do you expect that what happened to Jesus will one day be extended to you? Do you believe that in some mysterious way it is being extended to you even now through his Body, the Church?
4. Do you hope one day to see God face to face? Have you ever wondered what it will be like? Are there any images that come to mind?
5. What will you say to God when you finally meet him face to face? Will your words come from your mouth or from your heart? Will you be speechless? Will you simply reverence God in silence?
6. What will God say to you when you meet him face to face? Will you be afraid? Overcome with joy? A mixture of both?

Exercise

Sit alone in a dark room. Stay there in quiet for a few minutes. Then, look around you. What do you see? Probably not even your hands in front of you. Now strike a match and light a candle. Stare at the flame for a few moments. Take a good look at it. Watch it. Gaze upon it. Then look around and observe the great difference in what you see. Now reflect on this: Like the absence or presence of light, faith in the Risen Lord changes our perceptions of the world around us, of ourselves, and what it means to see God face to face.

Prayer to Mary

Mary, my mother,
And mother of my Lord,
I have always turned to you
In times of need—
And I do so now.
Help me to keep alive
The glowing embers
Of my faith,
Buried though they seem,
At times,
Beneath the smoldering ashes
Of doubt and unbelief.
Help me to fan them
Alive with hope
And to kindle them
Into a burning fire
Of love
That will purify
All within me
That holds me back
And keeps me
From following
The way
Of your Son.
Help me,
Dear mother,
Help me
To become a saint!

The Manner of Making Mental Prayer

By Saint Alphonsus de Liguori
(1696—1757)

The Preparation

Begin by disposing your mind and body to enter into pious recollection.

Leave at the door of the place where you are going to converse with God all extraneous thoughts, saying, with Saint Bernard, "O my thoughts! Wait here; after prayer we shall speak on other matters." Be careful not to allow the mind to wander where it wishes.

The posture of the body most suitable for prayer is to be kneeling; but if this posture becomes so irksome as to cause distractions, we may, as Saint John of the Cross says, make our meditation while sitting down.

The preparation consists of three acts: (1) Act of faith in the presence of God; (2) Act of humility and contrition; (3) Act of petition for light. We may perform these acts in the following manner:

Act of Faith in the Presence of God, and Act of Adoration

My God, I believe that you are here present, and I adore you with my whole soul.

(Be careful to make this act with a lively faith, for a lively remembrance of the divine presence contributes greatly to remove distractions. Cardinal Carracciolo, Bishop of Aversa, used to say that when a person is distracted in prayer there is reason to think that he has not made a lively act of faith.)

Act of Humility and of Contrition

Lord, I should now be in hell in punishment of the offenses I have given you. I am sorry for them from the bottom of my heart; have mercy on me.

Act of Petition for Light

Eternal Father, for the sake of Jesus and Mary, give me light in this meditation, that I may draw fruit from it.

Further Prayers

We must then recommend ourselves to the Blessed Virgin by saying a Hail Mary, to Saint Joseph, to our guardian angel, and to our holy patron.

These acts, says Saint Francis de Sales, ought to be made with fervor, but should be short, that we may pass immediately into the meditation.

The Meditation

When you make meditation privately you may always use some book, at least at the commencement, and stop when you find yourself most touched. Saint Francis de Sales says that in this we should do as the bees that stop on a flower as long as they find any honey in it, and then pass on to another. Saint Teresa of Avila used a book for seventeen years; she would first read a little, then meditate for a short time on what she had read. It is useful to meditate in this manner, in imitation of the pigeon that first drinks and then raises its eyes to heaven.

When mental prayer is made in common, one person reads for the rest the subject of meditation and divides it into two parts: the first is read at the beginning, after the preparatory acts; the second, towards the middle of the half hour. One should read in a loud tone of voice, and slowly, so as to be well understood.

It should also be remembered that the advantage of mental prayer consists not so much in meditating as in making affections, petitions, and resolutions: these are the three principal fruits of meditation. "The progress of a soul," says Saint Teresa of Avila, "does not consist in thinking much of God, but in loving him ardently; and this love is acquired by resolving to do a great deal for him."

Speaking of mental prayer, the spiritual masters say that meditation is, as it were, the needle which, when it is passed, must be succeeded by the golden thread, composed, as has been said, of affections, petitions, and resolutions; and this we are going to explain.

The Affections

When you have reflected on the point of meditation, and feel any pious sentiment, raise your heart to God and offer him acts of humility, of confidence, or of thanksgiving; but, above all, repeat in mental prayer acts of contrition and of love.

The act of love, as also the act of contrition, is the golden chain that brings the soul to God. An act of perfect charity is sufficient for the remission of all our sins: "For love covers a multitude of sins" (1 Pet 4:8). The Lord has declared that he cannot hate the soul that loves him: "I love those who love me" (Prov 8:17). The Venerable Sister Mary Crucified once saw a globe of fire, in which some straws that had been thrown into it were instantly consumed. By this vision she was given to understand that a soul, by making a true act of love, obtains the remission of all its faults. Besides, the angelic doctor teaches that by every act of love we acquire a new degree of glory. "Every act of charity merits eternal life."

Acts of love may be made in the following manner:

> My God, I esteem you more than all things.
> I love you with my whole heart.
> I delight in your felicity.
> I would wish to see you loved by all.
> I wish only what you wish.
> Make known to me what you wish from me,
> and I will do it.
> Dispose as you please of me and of all that I possess.

This last act of oblation is particularly dear to God.

In meditation, among the acts of love toward God, there is none more perfect than taking delight in the infinite joy of God. This is certainly the continual exercise of the blessed in heaven; so that he who often rejoices in the joy of God begins in this life to do that which he hopes to do in heaven through all eternity.

It may be useful here to remark, with Saint Augustine, that it is not torture, but the cause, which makes the martyr. Whence Saint Thomas teaches that martyrdom is to suffer death in the exercise of an act of virtue. From which we may infer that not only he who by hands of the executioner lays down his life for the faith, but whoever dies to comply with the divine will, and to please God, is a martyr, since in sacrificing himself to the divine love he performs an act of the most exalted virtue.

We all have to pay the great debt of nature; let us therefore endeavor, in holy prayer, to obtain resignation to the divine will—to receive death and every tribulation in conformity with the dispensations of his providence. As often as we perform this act of resignation with sufficient fervor, we may hope to be made partakers of the merits of the martyrs. Saint Mary Magdalene, in reciting the doxology, always bowed her head in the same spirit as she would have done in receiving the stroke of the executioner.

Remember that we here speak of the ordinary mental prayer; for should anyone feel himself at anytime united with God by supernatural or infused recollection, without any particular thought of an eternal truth or of any divine mystery, he should not then labor to perform any other acts than those to which he feels himself sweetly drawn to God. It is then enough to endeavor, with loving attention, to remain united with God, without impeding the divine operation, or forcing himself to make reflections and acts. But this is to be understood when the Lord calls the soul to this supernatural prayer; but until we receive such a call, we should not depart from the ordinary method of mental meditation and affections. However, for persons accustomed to mental prayer, it is better to employ themselves in affections than in consideration.

Petitions

Moreover, in mental prayer it is very profitable, and perhaps more useful than any other act, to repeat petitions to God, asking with humility and confidence, his graces; that is, his light, resignation, perseverance, and the like; but, above all, the gift of his holy love. Saint Francis de Sales used to say that by obtaining divine love we obtain all graces; for a soul that truly loves God with its whole heart will, of itself, without being admonished by others, abstain from giving him the smallest displeasure, and will labor to please him to the best of its ability.

When you find yourself in aridity and darkness, so that you feel, as it were, incapable of making good acts, it is sufficient to say: "My Jesus, mercy. Lord, for the sake of your mercy, assist me." And the meditation made in this manner will be for you perhaps the most useful and fruitful.

The Venerable Paul Segneri used to say that until he studied theology, he employed himself during the time of mental prayer in making reflections and affections; but "God" (these are his own words) "afterwards opened my eyes, and thenceforward I endeavored to employ myself in petitions; and if there is any good in me, I ascribe it to this exercise of recommending myself to God." You should likewise do the same; ask of God his graces in the name of Jesus Christ, and you will obtain whatsoever you desire. This our Savior has promised, and his promise cannot fail: "Whatever you ask the Father, he will give you in my name."

In a word, all mental prayer should consist in acts and petitions. Hence, the Venerable Sister Mary Crucified, while in an ecstasy, declared that mental prayer is the respiration of the soul; for, as by respiration the air is first attracted, and afterwards given back, so, by petitions the soul first receives grace from God, and then, by good acts of oblation and love, it gives itself to him.

Resolutions

In terminating the meditation, it is necessary to make a particular resolution; as, for example, to avoid some particular defect into which you have more frequently fallen, or to practice some virtue, such as to suffer the annoyance which you receive from another person, to obey more exactly a certain superior, to perform some particular act of mortification. We must repeat the same resolution several times, until we find that we have got rid of the defect or acquired the virtue. Afterwards reduce to practice the resolutions you have made, as soon as the occasion is presented. You would also do well, before the conclusion of your prayer, to renew the vows or any particular engagement by vow or otherwise that you have made with God; we multiply the merit of the good work, and draw down upon us a new help in order to persevere and to grow in grace.

The Conclusion

The conclusion of meditation consists of three acts:

1. In thanking God for the lights received;
2. In making a purpose to fulfill the resolutions made;
3. In asking of the Eternal Father, for the sake of
   Jesus and Mary, grace to be faithful to them.

Be careful never to omit, at the end of the meditation, to recommend to God the souls in purgatory and poor sinners. Saint John Chrysostom says that nothing more clearly shows our love for Jesus Christ than our zeal in recommending our brethren to him.

Saint Francis de Sales remarks that in leaving mental prayer we should take with us a nosegay of glowers in order to smell them during the day; in which we have felt particular devotion in order to excite our fervor during the day.

The ejaculations which are dearest to God are those of love, of resignation, of oblation of ourselves. Let us endeavor not to perform any action without first offering it to God, and not to allow at the most a quarter of an hour to pass, in whatever occupations we may find ourselves, without raising the heart to the Lord by some good act. Moreover, in our leisure time, such as when we are waiting for a person, or when we walk in the garden, or are confined to bed by sickness, let us endeavor, to the best of our ability, to unite ourselves to God. It is also necessary by observing silence, by seeking solitude as much as possible, and by remembering the presence of God, to preserve the pious sentiments conceived in meditation.

Appendix B
Speaking to God With Confidence and Familiarity
by Saint Alphonsus de Liguori
(1696—1787)

HOLY JOB WAS struck with wonder to consider our God so devoted in benefiting humans, and showing the chief care of his heart to love human beings and to make himself beloved by them. Speaking to the Lord, he exclaims: "What are human beings, that you make so much of them, that you set your mind on them?" (Job 7:17). Hence it is clearly a mistake to think the great confidence and familiarity in treating with God is a want of reverence to his Infinite Majesty. You ought indeed, O devout soul! to revere him in all humility, and abase yourself before him; especially when you call to mind the unthankfulness and the outrages of which, in past time, you have been guilty. Yet this should not hinder your treating him with the most tender love and confidence in your power. He is Infinite Majesty; but at the same time he is Infinite Goodness, Infinite Love. In God you possess the Lord most exalted and supreme; but you have also him who loves you with the greatest possible love. He disdains not, but delights that you should use towards him that confidence, that freedom and tenderness, which children use towards their mothers. Hear how he invites us to come to his feet, and the caresses he promises to bestow on us: "You shall nurse and be carried on her arm, and dandled on her knees. As a mother comforts her child, so I will comfort you" (Isa 66:12, 13). As a mother delights to place her little child upon her knees, and so to feed or to caress him; with like tenderness does our gracious God delight to treat the souls whom he loves, who have given

115

themselves wholly to him, and placed all their hopes in his goodness.

Consider, you have no friend nor brother, nor father nor mother, nor spouse nor lover, who loves you more than your God. The divine grace is that great treasure whereby we vilest of creatures, we servants, become the dear friends of our Creator himself: "For it is an unfailing treasure for mortals; those who get it obtain friendship with God" (Wis 7:14). For this purpose he increases our confidence; he is "being poured out" (Phil 2:7), and brought himself to nought, so to speak; abasing himself even to becoming man and conversing familiarly with us: "...and lived with humankind" (Bar 3:37). He went so far as to become an infant, to become poor, even so far as openly to die the death of a malefactor upon the cross. He went yet farther, even to hide himself under the appearance of bread, in order to become our constant companion and unite himself intimately to us: "Those who eat my flesh and drink my blood abide in me, and I in them. Just as the living Father sent me, and I live because of the Father, so whoever eats me will live because of me" (Jn 6:56–57). In a word, he loves you as much as though he had no love but toward yourself alone. For which reason you ought to have no love for any but for him. Of him, therefore, you may say, and you ought to say, "My beloved is mine and I am his" (Song 2:16). My God has given himself all to me, and I give myself all to him; he has chosen me for his beloved, and I choose him of all others, for my only Love: "My beloved is all radiant and ruddy, distinguished among ten thousand" (Song 5:10).

Say, then, to him often, "O my Lord! why do you love me so? what good thing do you see in me? Have you forgotten the injuries I have done you? But since you have treated me so lovingly, and instead of casting me into hell, have granted me so many favors, whom can I desire to love from this day forward but you, my God, my all? Ah, most gracious God, if in time past I have offended you, it is not so much the punishment I have deserved that now grieves me, as the displeasure I have given you, who are worthy of infinite love. But you know not how to despise a heart that repents and humbles itself": "A broken and contrite heart, O God, you will not despise" (Ps 51:17). Ah, now, indeed, neither in this life nor in the other do I desire any but you alone: "Whom have I in heaven but you? And there is nothing on earth that I desire other than you. My flesh and my heart may fail, but God is the strength of my heart and my portion forever" (Ps 73:25–26). You alone are and shall be forever the only Lord of my heart, of my will; you my only good, my heaven, my hope, my love, my all: "God is the strength of my heart and my portion forever."

The more to strengthen your confidence in God, often call to mind his loving treatment of you, and the gracious means he has used to drive you from the disorders of your life and your attachments to earth in order to draw you to his holy love; and therefore fear to have too little confidence in treating with your God, now that you have a resolute will to love and to please him with all your power. The mercies he has granted you are most sure pledges of the love he bears you. God is displeased with a want of trust on the part of souls that heartily love him, and whom he loves. If, then, you desire to please his loving heart, converse with him from this day forward with the greatest confidence and tenderness you can possibly have.

"See, I have inscribed you on the palms of my hands; your walls are continually before me" (Isa 49:16). Beloved soul, says the Lord, what do you fear and mistrust? I have you written in my hands, so as never to forget to do you good. Are you afraid of your enemies? Know that the care of your defense is always before me, so that I cannot lose sight of it. Therefore did David rejoice, saying to God, "You cover them with favor as with a shield" (Ps 5:12). Who, O Lord! can ever harm us, if you with your goodness and love defend and encompass us roundabout? Above all, animate your confidence at the thought of the gift that God has given us of Jesus Christ: "For God so loved the world that he gave his only Son" (Jn 3:16). How can we ever fear, exclaims the Apostle, that God would refuse us any good, after he has vouchsafed to give us his only Son? "He who did not withhold his own Son, but gave him up for all of us, will he not with him also give us everything else?" (Rom 8:32).

"I was daily his delight, delighting in the human race" (Prov

8:30). The paradise of God, so to speak, is the heart of man. Does God love you? Love him. His delights are to be with you; let yours be to be with him, to pass all your lifetime with him, in the delight of whose company you hope to spend a blissful eternity. Accustom yourself to speak with him alone, familiarly, with confidence and love, as to the dearest friend you have, and who loves you best.